★

CH★RLIE MIKE

Glenda Hyde
With Ben Flores
And The Boys' Parents

AuthorHouse™
1663 Liberty Drive
Bloomington, IN 47403
www.authorhouse.com
Phone: 833-262-8899

Because of the dynamic nature of the Internet, any web addresses or links contained in this book may have changed since publication and may no longer be valid. The views expressed in this work are solely those of the author and do not necessarily reflect the views of the publisher, and the publisher hereby disclaims any responsibility for them.

The front cover image was donated by Christy Fatula, owner of Hold You Me Studios.

New International Version (NIV) Holy Bible, New International Version®, NIV® Copyright ©1973, 1978, 1984, 2011 by Biblica, Inc.® Used by permission. All rights reserved worldwide.

This book is printed on acid-free paper.

ISBN: 978-1-6655-6707-7 (sc)
ISBN: 978-1-6655-6787-9 (hc)
ISBN: 978-1-6655-6708-4 (e)

Print information available on the last page.

Published by AuthorHouse 08/18/2022

authorHOUSE®

The public release clearance of this publication by the Department of Defense does not imply Department of Defense endorsement or factual accuracy of the material.

The true soldier fights, not because he hates what is in front of him, but because he loves what is behind him.

G.K. Chesterton

Also by Glenda Hyde

24 Years and 40 Days: The Story of Army 1LT Daniel Hyde

TABLE OF CONTENTS

For the boys and their parents, all of whom I am honored to know:

Daniel John
Caden Daniel
Daniel Benjamin
Nicolas Hyde
Jordan Daniel
Owen Daniel
Anakin Hyde
Jayce Daniel
Daniel Edward
Caleb Daniel
Kenneth Daniel
Daniel Roy
Elliott Daniel
And
Hudson Daniel

Thank you is completely inadequate!

ACKNOWLEDGEMENTS:

I give my utmost thanks and gratitude to my sister, Brenda. I did not appreciate her enough when I was younger.

By the time she was 36, she had been teaching elementary school for 10 years, given birth to **four** boys (a baby, an 18-month-old, a three-year-old and a five-year-old), and was finishing her Doctorate in Administration, Curriculum, and Teaching Studies at UCLA.

I was 35 with two kids, doing part-time in-home day care, and thought I was busy.

I remember sitting at her graduation from UCLA thinking, my sister has a PhD. She has gone **all the way** in education.

Brenda is one of the most intelligent people I know. Her husband has a doctorate in Medieval History, and all **four** of their boys are college graduates. This is an accomplished family, and humble, all of them.

Brenda must have sprinkled my baby boy with "love of learning" fairy dust because Daniel did NOT get his love of learning from either of his parents.

I could not have completed my books without Brenda's profound assistance.

Great thanks to the boys' parents, Jim and Annette, and Derek and Jenny for sharing your relationship to Daniel with me and allowing me to tell these beautiful stories.

Thank you, Ali, for encouraging me to add stories that deepen one's understanding of Daniel and broaden the scope of his legacy.

And Ben, thank you for your journal entries years ago and your willingness to continue writing. Thank you for suggesting the perfect book title, and partnering with me in this endeavor to celebrate Daniel and his legacy through all of us.

To all who proofread, I appreciate your fresh eyes and your contribution.

PREFACE

He was a stand-up guy: Smart, athletic, kind, and humble. He embodied the qualities of a balanced young man. His friend, Derek, described him as COMPLETE and a BADASS. His favorite mentor and coach, Bill McHale, said he was motivated, but relaxed; driven, but never aggressive; competitive, but always a sportsman; always busy, but never complaining; a gentle soul, but a passionate soldier. With all he was capable of during his short time on earth, it was his character that made him special.

As his high school's quarterback, he took hit after hit, always returning to the huddle encouraging his team that a win was still within reach. In basketball, he would make the pass and be happy with the assist. A four-year, three-sport athlete, twice elected Student Body President, with a flawless GPA, on his way to West Point during a war. What gave him his drive?

He became part of the Long Gray Line and during his time at the United States Military Academy he continued to accept no mediocrity. Grades and leadership remained his top priorities. He was never willing to take the shortcuts that would make his life easier but would stray from his values. He loved completing problem sets first so that he could offer help to fellow engineering peers.

He willingly participated in land navigation drills and mask removal in the gas chamber along with the younger cadets while serving as their BEAST Commander. During BEAST, slang for cadet basic training at West Point, the new cadets are required to remove their mask briefly and answer a couple of questions in the gas chamber, thus allowing them to inhale a small amount of gas. This exercise will instill in them the importance of chemical gear. It was not required of the BEAST Commander, however, to hear that he willingly participated with the young new cadets was not surprising.

He tackled one of his most challenging obstacles by completing Ranger School.

A recycle in Ranger School is horrible although it happens to many soldiers at least once. The most difficult part of the recycle is that there is no indication from the Ranger Instructors (RI) regarding what one needs to "fix." The RIs simply say pass or fail with no explanation given. Therefore, it is nearly impossible for the Ranger student to work on their shortcomings because they do not know what they are. It is devastating because all you know is you failed and you will be repeating a 21-day cycle with not much food, very little sleep, and drills and challenges that take you to places you do not want to go.

Recycling *twice* meant FOUR months of this exhausting, frustrating, dirty, cold, hungry, infuriating, madness. This is the reason only about half of the soldiers that begin Ranger School will finish and receive their Ranger tab.

With his legendary perseverance even after *two recycles* he was eventually awarded his Ranger tab followed by his Airborne wings.

He was on a mission.

Did he know his days were numbered?

His family hoped that finally he could start living, but duty called too soon. He tried to comfort those around him by explaining he was trained and ready for whatever lay ahead. In the Fall of 2008, he left for the hot dusty sands of Iraq and five short months later his military escort and friend, Ben Flores, brought him home.

While this could read as a short story thankfully it is not. Instead, it is the beginning of a beautiful legacy that continues to unfold...

AUTHOR'S NOTE

My original intention in writing *Charlie Mike*, a term used in the military that translates to **continue mission,** was simply to share the stories of 14 boys and their parents who chose to name a child in honor and remembrance of Daniel. Fourteen boys that will in one way or another continue Daniel's mission. Though each story is unique, and the boys' and their parents' stories could stand alone, other notable events have taken place that I wanted to share.

Dorothy Parker, a medical procedures specialist at Daniel's elementary school, who is a faithful supporter of all things Daniel, suggested that because of this book maybe the boys could somehow become connected. Perhaps someday they would like to form a reunion of sorts and get to know one another, since they all have ONE common thread in Daniel.

I asked Ben Flores to continue writing. He had emailed me three journal entries years ago explaining how he was chosen to be Daniel's military escort. He had planned to record the entire process but stopped the night before receiving Daniel and meeting our family in Modesto. He mentioned that he wished he would have continued writing.

The escort process has been performed thousands of times in the past 20 years. However, not much is known about it. I personally wanted to know the entire process, how Ben was impacted by it, and how his life is affected today, as he continues his service in the Army.

Charlie Mike.

BEN FLORES, ESCORT ENTRIES

The following pages are entries from Major Benjamin Flores. Ben was asked to escort Daniel home from Dover Air Force Base in Dover, Delaware. All deceased overseas military persons reenter the United States through Dover Air Force Base where they are prepared for burial. Then they are flown to their hometown lying in a flag-covered casket accompanied by their Military Escort.

Ben was a classmate of Daniel's at West Point and at the time of his escort duty Ben was 24 and a 1st Lieutenant in the United States Army.

Glenda,

I finished your book yesterday and, as promised, I have your gift. Attached are three journal entries I wrote while I was on escort duty for Dan. I originally intended to write down my experiences through the entire process, but I stopped the day before I met you in Modesto. Right now, I am wishing I had not. At any rate no one has ever read these. I think my original intent was to maybe publish the account, or at a minimum, share them with Dan's family. I had known about *Taking Chance*, the new movie starring Kevin Bacon, about a military escort. I can't tell you why I've sat on these for so long, but after finally reading your book, I feel the time is right to pass these on to you so you can know how I felt before I walked off that plane into yours and your family's lives.

It was quite the struggle to experience everything again reading your book. I'm pretty sure I went through the five stages of grief all over again. I guess in many ways I've repressed a lot of the emotions because Dan's death is still something very painful for me. Sure, I still wear his KIA bracelet every day, but I hardly take the time to think about the man whose name is etched on it. Your book forced me to do just that, and I am so appreciative for it. Not only did I feel the sorrow again over his loss, but I spent a lot of time thinking about how great Dan was and about the time we spent together. I remember a lot from right before he left Hawaii mostly because it was one of the best monthslong stretches in my life. We were young, living in Hawaii, and partying like rock stars.

And while most of my memories revolve around us going out and having a good time, the one I cherish the most regarding Dan was in church. R.J. posted a photo of that day on Facebook - the one where you said Danny and I were twins. In our defense those were our club clothes from the night prior. Party hard Saturday night and repent on Sunday. So that day was R.J., Danny, and Dan's last Sunday church before deploying and the church decided to do this big ceremony for us to bless us and request God's protection over the deployment. They brought the four of us on stage, sang and prayed and asked God over and over to look after us. They then blessed us all with some kind of oil and poured it all over the stage. To be honest it all seemed corny, and I was pretty uncomfortable, but I went with it because I figured God's protection couldn't hurt as I would deploy shortly after them.

After the ceremony they asked us all to go around and embrace each other and the well-wishers around the church and give each other words of encouragement or something like that. I don't remember a damn thing that anybody said to me or wished me that day, but I do remember what Dan said after we gave each other a hug. He gave me this very satisfied smile - it wasn't the big Dan Hyde smile everyone talks about but almost a smirk - and said, "I'm glad you're here." I remember being so in awe of him at that moment. I've never been much of the religious type and Dan knew that, but I felt he wanted to make a point that I was at the right place that Sunday morning. He made me feel so comfortable and glad I was at church. He didn't proselytize like a lot of my other Christian friends who tried to convert me. Nor did he pass judgment or dig into what the deal was with my faith. He simply offered four words that reached me spiritually more than the thousands of, quite frankly, wasted words of others. No one has reached me like that since and come to think of it, that was the last time I went to a Sunday church service.

Thank you for writing your book, for showing your more vulnerable side throughout it, and forcing me to mourn, remember, and reflect. Another great thing about your book is the inclusion of how others felt and how similar their words were to my own thoughts. The one that resonated the most was from one of Dan's privates, who explained why such a terrible thing had happened by saying that God took the very best to make his angels. I still wouldn't call myself a Christian, but I know that is true. You rock, Glenda.

Much love.
- Ben

DAY 1: SHOCK

Well, here I am in the air heading towards Philadelphia to escort my dear friend Dan Hyde back home. It is crazy to think that I had no idea I was going to be Dan's official escort until about 24 hours ago. While I knew about the escort duty, I was told that Danny Hwang – my old team leader from West Point – would have the honor of doing it. I was pleased to know that although I would not be there for Dan, a close friend would be. Knowing this, I went ahead and wrote Danny an email thanking him for escorting Dan and even expressed my desire to be there alongside him.

Despite finding comfort in knowing that Danny would be seeing Dan home, there was a part of me that yearned to have the opportunity to be Dan's escort and see him to his final resting place. Dan was a great man – probably the greatest man I will ever know – and a dear friend. I worked directly for him as his regimental executive officer (XO) at school where we became friends and during that time, I gained immense respect for him. I had hung out with him in Hawaii prior to his deployment. I even got to drop off Dan at Schofield to be deployed to Iraq. I hoped to pick him up upon redeployment (the return of the deployed unit). There is still a part of me that doesn't want to believe that Dan will never be coming back to Hawaii.

When I found out about Dan, I was in shock and utter disbelief. While it wasn't ideal, I found out about Dan through Facebook this past Sunday. I had just driven back home late that morning following a night on the town down in Waikiki. Upon returning home, I went through my usual routine of checking my Facebook. While checking my friends' statuses, I saw what would bring my upbeat and optimistic world (I had returned from Iraq just a week and a half prior) down. A mutual friend posted something along the lines of, "Dan, we love you and we will miss you."

Knowing this friend was in 3rd Brigade and that there were two other Dans I knew there, all I could think was, "Just don't let it be Dan Hyde."

I checked Dan's Facebook profile and with all the messages posted to him, it became ever apparent as to what had happened.

Sitting there with my roommates watching T.V. I blurted out, "Dan Hyde got killed." My roommate Chip Teets – another classmate of ours – turned off the T.V. There was silence. Chip got up, went to his room and in utter disbelief I went to the kitchen to make lunch.

In the kitchen, I just stood there. Without any purpose or direction, I wandered the kitchen opening various drawers thinking about the news I just read. After about five minutes, it finally hit me and it became very real. I went back into the living room, sat down, and began to cry. I cried because at that point I realized I would never see Dan again. How could this happen to Dan? He was the most solid guy I knew from school. I had talked to him less than a week ago. There seemed to be no hope when a guy like Dan Hyde gets killed overseas. The world suffered a huge loss.

Still crying, Chip came to me and brought me into his room so he could calm me down. Sitting on his bed all I could say was, "What the fuck?" Repeatedly I said it. I mean, what do you say when you find out the friend you admired the most was killed in a war that seemed to be winding down? Chip and I talked for a while and I did calm down, but I was still in shock. There was this utter feeling of hopelessness and helplessness that I had never felt before.

The thought of Dan being gone has been with me constantly all week and that helpless feeling continues to linger. There has been this feeling of anxiousness all week to help however I can. Dan was always willing to help others. I wanted to be more like Dan.

Through a couple of occurrences, an Army regulation that makes no sense, and good timing, I am now the official escort for Dan. Danny was not allowed to be the escort because, for some unknown reason, the Army has a regulation stating that soldiers from the same unit cannot serve as escorts.

With Danny out, the escort duty was going to be given to a captain who had never met Dan. It just so happened that this captain was expecting his family to visit him in Hawaii for the week he would have to serve as escort. I called Captain Sofge, the 2-35 Infantry rear detachment commander regarding Dan's memorial service at Schofield. This is when he explained the entire situation and propositioned me with being Dan's official escort.

Despite having plans for the upcoming week, my roommate had three girls visiting and staying at our house for spring break, I accepted the escort duty. I know Dan would have wanted a friend to be there for him, and with Danny out of the picture I would now be that friend. A small part of me wanted to take the easy way out and stay in Hawaii, with the girls, and avoid the emotional ride I was about to go on. However, I don't think I'd be able to live with myself if I refused to be Dan's escort because I know Dan would have done the same thing for me. Even if Dan had had a hot date with the bartender at The Yard House he was ever so fond of, I know he would have been there for me. Dan was the definition of selfless.

I find it funny how things of great importance in my life always seem to work themselves out. Although I've never really considered myself a religious man, I know in my heart that The Lord is at work here. I've been struggling ever since I found out about Dan and have felt guilty for not being able to do something. I see this as God's way of helping me get through this and giving me the chance to be there for Dan like he was there for me and others so many times. I am sure with Dan in mind, God made this happen. There is no other way to explain how all the pieces fell into place.

So now here I am on my way to receive Dan and be with him on his final flight home. I am not sure how I'm going to deal with this whole process. I have been warned that it will be emotionally draining, but I don't care. I'm glad I was given this opportunity.

I am sure Dan is smiling from above knowing that a friend – who has struggled with coming to terms with his death – is serving as his escort. I hope this process helps me find peace and helps me become a better person.

What an amazing spirit. Even in death, Dan is still lending help to a friend.

DAY 2: ARRIVAL

I arrived at the Philadelphia International Airport around 0900 this morning. Upon arrival, I was feeling the six hours' time difference. I got about two hours of sleep on the plane ride over and my plans of renting a car to visit friends in either D.C. or New York were scrapped, because all I want to do is sleep!

When I got to the hotel (the luxurious Ramada Inn) and said I was military, they knew exactly why I was there. It seems that all the military escorts come through this hotel. The girl at the front desk was nice about everything and tried to give me a room where things would be quiet. Apparently, there was a Mason convention going on that day so she wanted to make sure that I wouldn't be disturbed by any crazy rituals. By crazy rituals I mean drunk and rambunctious Masons playing their rap music too loud. After getting to my room, I went to bed and slept until about 5 in the afternoon. The time difference was hitting me.

When I woke from my slumber, I couldn't help but think about Dan and the task I'm about to partake in. Whenever I see people acting in a disrespectful or inappropriate manner, I think about how Dan would act in a similar situation. At the Philly Cheese Steak restaurant where I grabbed dinner, there was a confrontation between a customer and the cashier. Dan was always so polite about everything even if he didn't have to be. It was amazing to see Dan treat everyone with respect even if I felt that they didn't deserve to be treated so. I don't think I ever heard Dan talk bad about a single person at school. I know I certainly talked bad about some to him.

Although I haven't done exceptionally well at it, I've been trying to treat others like Dan would, since his passing.

Obviously, there are a whole lot of people who irritate me, but I know in my heart that talking bad about them or disrespecting them will bring about nothing positive. That is probably why Dan never did such things. That is just one of the things I know I need to start doing to go along with the desired "live more like Dan Hyde."

While sitting in my room I watched about half of *Saving Private Ryan*. I hadn't seen the movie in a while. During some parts I had to turn the channel, though. The parts about Ryan's brothers never coming home and "making the ultimate sacrifice" proved to be too much for me. It's strange how things that would never have bothered me two weeks ago, now seem very real and very sad.

I am sure I will encounter many things like this for the rest of my life, after my journey with Dan ends.

It just dawned on me, the burden I am about to take on. I am escorting the "remains" of a close friend and a great American, home. I hate that damned word… "remains." It is so impersonal, so cold. Despite him being gone in person, I am still referring to Dan as Dan. It is only fair to someone whose spirit still lives and continues to inspire me.

I know things are going to be difficult over the next couple days, but I am still glad that I'll be able to do this for Dan.

DAY 3: STILL WAITING

Tomorrow's the day everything starts, and I don't think I realize what I'm getting into. It's easy enough to agree to this escorting business for Dan and his family but will I be able to hold up? Will I be strong? My current state is calm but that could all change tomorrow when I come face to face with Dan's flag-draped casket. I hope I stay strong. I guess tomorrow will tell.

Today was just more waiting around, more avoidance of thought on the task at hand. I did make time for some reflection today. During lunch I thought about how every action, every little occurrence, leads to this exact point in time. Although I know I'm not ultimately responsible, I thought how things that have happened in the past year for me could have somehow led to Dan's death.

I was supposed to be in 2-35 Infantry with Dan, but the Army switched me to 2nd Brigade when I got to Hawaii. Had I gone to 2-35 would things be different? Would Dan still be alive? Would I be in the place of Dan right now? Would we both return to Hawaii safely this upcoming October?

I know no good can come of dwelling on these questions, but I can't help but have my mind wander. Just to look back and see all the events that led me to not going to 2-35. First, there was the stress fracture I got in the summer of 2007 that pushed back the start of my training to October. The majority of my classmates started in July and August. Then there was my hip injury that prevented me from starting Ranger School May 5, so I started May 26 instead.

Then there is my recycling Ranger School which pushed my timeline back another six weeks. By the time I left Fort Benning, it was already September. I got to Hawaii in October and at that point it seemed that 3rd Brigade had no need for me, so they sent me to 2nd Brigade to deploy for three and a half months and see no action. I guess things turned out all right for me in the end, but I can't help but feel guilty for having things the way they are.

One can only think about what could have been, had any of those events happened differently. You never know, things could still be the way they are right now. I guess it's all part of God's plan as to why things are the way they are. Now it's up to me to make sense of this whole thing and find purpose in the way things have transpired. Dan served his purpose. Now I must find mine…

Well, I should get to bed.

Big day tomorrow.

★

DAY 4: HOME

With *the* day having arrived, I found myself oddly focused as I prepared for what lay ahead. I certainly was still feeling the weight of what I was about to do, but I wasn't exactly sad like I had been the previous days. I was more anxious and nervous about how the day would go, yet determined to do it right. My demeanor was not too different from how I felt prior to a patrol in Iraq. I had a mission to accomplish, and I was ready to execute despite my reservations. As I put on my green service uniform it dawned on me that the uniform I associated with celebration – most notably my graduation from West Point – and the prestige of the military, would now also represent sorrow and sacrifice. I collected my things, checked out of the room, and boarded a shuttle for Dover Air Force Base. It was time to take Dan home.

I arrived at Dover's mortuary affairs office and the non-commissioned officer there brought me inside and briefed me on my mission. During the brief, he provided a folder with administrative paperwork, which displayed the full name and rank of both Dan and myself. It was a blast from the past to see our names on the folder together as they were, considering our names had been in close proximity so many times while at West Point. We were the #1 and #2 ranking cadet officers in our regiment. A hint of nostalgia passed over me as my brief continued.

As part of the brief, I also received a small bag with the possessions that were on Dan's person when he died. The bag included his dog tags – the ones we've all seen in the movies of the soldiers that didn't make it – and his watch. In typical Army fashion there was a formal procedure for receiving and accounting for his effects. I had to take each item out of the bag, verify that it was on the paperwork I received, and verbally tell the soldier that I had physical possession of the item. In addition to the bag of personal items, I also received ten pendants and most importantly, the key to the casket.

With the briefing complete, my mission and purpose for the day were clear: I would receive Dan, confirm that it was him by checking the dog tags attached to his casket, maintain accountability of him during the flight home – to the point that I would recheck the tags at every stop on the way – and ensure delivery of him and his effects to his family in Modesto. While my nerves had calmed slightly after the brief, I was still anxious, wondering how I would react to seeing the flag-draped casket for the first time.

The moment of truth came when they called me outside informing me of Dan's arrival. I walked out and saw the white van that brought him back to me, just not like we had planned. I was the one who dropped him off to deploy in Hawaii. I can still remember telling him to "Be Safe" like we tell each other as if it actually offers some shield of protection, and how I would pick him up when he got back from Iraq. I guess I was picking him up like I said I would. The back of the van opened, and the mortuary affairs team brought Dan out, in his flag-draped coffin, like they must have done so many times.

I felt very little when I saw it. My mind was spinning with what lay before me - "Holy shit, Dan's in there. He's really in there. He's really gone. He's dead." – but I was in complete control of my emotions and my body. The literal training I had just received during my in-brief seemed to kick in. I coolly and calmly walked up to the casket to inspect the tags attached to the end to verify that my friend was in fact in there – *Hyde, Daniel*. It was Dan. I confirmed to the team that it was the right person and they loaded him up on the small charter plane that would bring him home.

I entered the small plane and sat down in my seating row up by the pilots. Right behind me was Dan. Much like when I first saw the casket, there was this certain detachment I felt towards what was to my rear and what I would turn around and look at periodically throughout the flight. I met the pilots, who seemed nice. I asked if they had done something like this before and they said they had. That was more or less the extent of the conversation. Perhaps I should have asked how they felt about everything – about taking the fallen home to their families; about the war; if they were uncomfortable or sad; if they knew the names of their precious cargo; if they often reflected on what they did. At any rate, they handed me a headset and I got to listen in on their transmission with the aircraft controllers. *Kalitta 1299* was our call sign. Cleared for takeoff, Dan and I were on our way home to California.

The flight was largely uneventful. I listened in on the traffic and learned how air traffic controllers and pilots navigated flights, but mostly took interest in the pilot's cadence signing in and out with *ka-let-ta twelve nine-nine* during transmissions. Every so often I glanced behind me at the box shaped American flag. The whole time it occurred to me that Dan was just behind me, in his casket, yet I was still surprisingly calm. I felt like I should have been more frazzled or sad or nervous like I was in the morning, but I wasn't. We stopped twice along the way, once outside St. Louis and later in Arizona. I disembarked both times. Upon reentering the aircraft, I checked the tags, as was my duty: *Hyde, Daniel*. With the last stop complete and tags verified, I ensured Dan would come home.

As we made our descent towards Modesto, the calm I had been experiencing since I walked into the mortuary affairs office at Dover began to come undone. I was more anxious. My heart rate was up. The time for the hard part of the job was upon me — deliver Dan to his family. As the airfield at the Modesto airport came into view, and I saw the crowds of people awaiting Dan's arrival lined up parallel to the runway, a wave of emotion came over me. The dam had broken on what I had bottled up the entire day and my face, throat, and body convulsed to cry. And then I saw them, Dan's family — Glenda, Brian, and Andrea — far out in front of the crowd, waiting. At this point I was at a near panic, and I knew I had to get it together. I imagined whatever I was feeling paled in comparison to what the Hydes were feeling in that same moment.

The plane touched down and my mind took over to get me under control. I began controlling my breathing and rehearsing in my head what I would do when I got off the plane and what I would say. I was merely a side character in Dan's journey home and wanted to make sure I executed my role in a dignified and professional manner as was expected of a military escort. Knowing Dan like I did, it was all very personal, but it could not be so in this moment.

I waited in my seat for several minutes in silence as the crew prepared to download Dan. The wait had allowed me to compose myself, to get it together, and I was as ready as I was going to be. I felt the sorrow and the grief and the weight of what I was about to do to my core, but I put on the face of the stoic soldier prepared to do his duty. The door finally opened and just outside was the Casualty Assistance Officer (CAO), Captain Bruce Corum, to greet me and instruct me on what was next.

I disembarked the plane with a somber look on my face, head, and eyes forward, hands cupped, shoulders straight, and marched over to the Hydes.

Focused on the task at hand, I greeted the Hydes. We hugged. I told them I was sorry and most importantly, I told them that Dan was home. They were extremely warm and welcoming, thus easing some of the tension I had built up not wanting to disappoint. I could sense their deep sorrow, but there was also a certain resolve that despite their world being completely shattered, they were standing there strong and composed. Maybe like me, they were keeping it all together, just barely, for the sake of appearances, not wanting to detract from Dan's final homecoming. We stood there silently waiting as they downloaded Dan from the plane.

I watched as Glenda, Brian, and Andrea approached Dan. It was a touching, moving, and heartbreaking affair. They clung closely together and looked upon their son and brother. I observed tender love and unfathomable grief mixed together as they gazed at the flag-draped casket. Andrea kissed her brother through the cold metal. It was a beautiful moment, yet it filled me with more sadness than I had experienced up to that point. I had fulfilled my duty to bring Dan home to them, but I found myself wishing that I could somehow do more.

After the Hydes had their time with Dan out on the tarmac, he was moved to the hearse to be transported to the funeral home. As the escort, I entered the vehicle to travel with him as I would until he was buried. At this point I was in a daze. I had mustered all my strength to keep it together at the airport and I was now spent. The day had taken an emotional toll on me, and it was still not over. After all, I was there for the Hydes, and I had to make sure they had everything they needed. We arrived at the funeral home, and I conducted my final check: *Hyde, Daniel.*

Still in somewhat of a daze, I entered the funeral home to continue my duty. I brought in Dan's effects, the ten pendants, and paperwork for the CAO and me to fill out. I entered the small room with the Hydes and Bruce, and met the replacement CAO, Major Desiree Soumoy. At this point we got down to business. We talked logistics and scheduling for the week, laying out the necessary administrative details for burying Dan as the funeral director situated him in the home. I mostly stayed quiet, I was exhausted, but I also did not want to speak out of turn. Observing everyone it was clear Glenda was in control of the situation despite the very real trauma she had been dealing with. Again, I could not help but admire her strength and calm.

After talking some more, the casket was set in place, and it was time for the family to spend time with Dan in a more personal setting. Glenda said she wanted to see him and asked if she could. The casualty paperwork I had in my packet described Dan as "unviewable" meaning his injuries were so severe, his body was in no condition to be viewed. The CAOs said they would inspect Dan to confirm what kind of condition he was in. I watched from afar as they went into the viewing room to see how he looked. After a brief moment the CAOs returned almost excited to tell us that Dan was in great shape, and we could see him. Glenda perked up, eager and relieved that she could see her son. With the thumbs up, we approached Dan to finally *see* him.

When I arrived at the open casket and viewed Dan's lifeless body, dressed in Army Greens with the new awards he received for dying in combat, I broke. I lost control and composure and quickly retreated to the first row of benches in the room. Andrea followed behind. The façade of the strong soldier doing his duty, that I had barely been keeping together that day, had completely crumbled. I sobbed, uncontrollably – the kind of heavy cry where in the moment there seems to be absolutely no hope. Sitting next to me, gently weeping, Andrea put her arm around me to comfort me in my grief. It was a nice moment of sorrow the two of us shared, but I couldn't help but feel guilty and selfish that she was the one comforting me and not the other way around.

I calmed down a bit and glanced up and viewed Brian and Glenda's gaze upon their son. They were both emotional, weeping softly, Brian more so, as they looked at Dan's body – his "vessel" as Glenda would later call it. There was a composure to Glenda as she stood there, sweetly looking at her son and gently caressing his face. It was a stark contrast to my reaction, and it provided me some resolve in the moment. Despite me being a complete wreck, I cannot begin to imagine what Glenda and Brian were feeling in that moment as Dan's parents. It was pure love and sadness and relief. Relief that their son was home, even if it was just his vessel. The calm and grace displayed by Glenda in that moment must have been a product of that relief. Dan, her son, was finally home.

The viewing concluded, the casket was closed, and we began discussing what was next. We talked the itinerary for the next few days, more logistics, and dinner plans. Glenda asked what was next for me. Still reeling from everything, I told her whatever she needed me for. Without missing a beat, Glenda told me I would be going home to Fresno for the next two days and would come back for the official visitation. She was adamant that my mom needed to see me. Not in a position to argue, I said okay. The Hydes finalized a place for dinner with the CAOs and we left the funeral home, and Dan, under darkness to get something to eat.

Dinner was nice given the circumstances. We chit-chatted and talked about Dan. Glenda and the CAOs talked the most, with Brian, Andrea, and me being more withdrawn. I was not in a talkative mood, but I engaged in conversation when appropriate. It came up that I had met the Hydes before while at West Point. It was during Ring Weekend in the fall of 2006. Dan and I were heading out to formation when our families met. The conversation was light, and we talked mostly about us all being from California's Central Valley. A happier time when we were all blissfully ignorant of how our paths would cross again under the most tragic of circumstances.

There was a certain surrealness to it all as we sat there and ate and conversed. We were doing routine things, going about our business, ordering appetizers and drinks – *living* – and it just did not seem right, but there we were. What else were we to do? I imagine all of us sitting there were contemplating this on some level. We all had had quite the day. Dan was dead, his death confirmed despite already knowing it to be true. The questions of "why" and all the emotions were probably at their rawest today. We were all grieving, but each of us dealing with it in our own way. Yet, we did have each other even if Dan was gone. Maybe carrying on and doing routine things, together, was the best thing we could do in that moment.

We finished dinner and the longest of days was finally coming to its conclusion. We all went outside and reviewed the next several days. My role and purpose came up again in conversation. I wanted to make sure that the Hydes knew that I was 100% there for them and I would do whatever they needed. It was irrelevant that I was close to home. I was not back in California to visit family. Again, and this time more firmly, Glenda told me to go home. She mentioned that she would want to see Dan had the roles been reversed. And with that, I didn't need to hear anything else.

Standing in the parking lot, we said goodbye, we hugged again, and we thanked one another. We had all been through a lot together over the course of the day and I would leave feeling a closeness with the Hyde family. In just a few hours, I felt that I truly got to know them. They are an amazing family and just plain good people. Their love, kindness, decency, and character were on full display along with a vulnerability that brought us all together. I always admired Dan because of his character. He was kind, respectful, caring, modest, and good at what seemed like everything – the greatest person I have ever known. It is clear from where he got it.

I got in Bruce's car, as he had agreed to drive me home, and we made the 90 mile drive down CA-99 to Fresno. We talked most of the way back about life and the Army, and largely avoided talking about the day's events. I was emotionally exhausted. I could tell Bruce was tired too. Being a CAO is no easy task and I respected him for being that professional military figure I had hoped but failed to be. I mean I had just brought my dead friend home to his family. Maybe I deserve some grace.

Bruce pulled up to my home and I gathered all my things that I had carried from Hawaii to Dover to Modesto and back home. I said goodbye to Bruce and walked up the driveway towards the front door. It was the first time I was home since I deployed to Iraq, and everything looked the same but felt different. The familiarity of it all blended with what I had experienced in Iraq and over the course of the day. As I approached the door, my mom opened it and came outside. She looked happy to see me. We embraced and she told me she was glad I was home. I choked up but was too tired to cry or say much of anything. We stood there out in front, holding on to each other.

Based on the embrace and the way my mom looked at me, I could sense the utter relief she felt as a mother. Her son was home from the war. He was alive. Never mind the phone call she received when I first returned from Iraq. I was there in the flesh, breathing and talking, confirming to her that I made it. It was a stark contrast to what Glenda experienced, yet similar in its own way. The entire day, Glenda had held it all together, showing a strength and resolve to calm *all* of us and here my mom was doing the same exact thing for her grief-stricken, emotionally exhausted son. My mom has always been very emotional, but on this day, through her measured emotions, she communicated in a way only a mother can – it will be all right.

The day was over. Dan was home. I was home. Our mothers welcomed us home. They gazed upon their beautiful boys and cared for us as only a mother could. In a way, we were all whole again, but one in life and the other in death.

★

DAY 5 & 6: WAITING

I spent the 17th and 18th at home between my parents' houses in Fresno largely recuperating. After going through the emotional ringer on the 16th, it was a nice reprieve from the weight I had felt since I agreed to serve as Dan's escort. I had the opportunity to catch up with my parents and more or less lounge around waiting for the next event centered on the fact that Dan was dead. During my time at home, a close friend and West Point classmate of mine, and a friend of Dan's, James Kelly, arrived in Fresno to pay his respects. He stayed with me at my dad's house. To pass the time, and probably to cope with our recent loss, we went out to a couple bars in town. Normally I would relish the opportunity to show a close friend of mine my hometown, but it was more about going through the motions as we waited for what lay ahead.

DAY 7: VISITATION

After the two-day break at home, I was back to facing Dan's death head on. Thursday was the public visitation and, once again, it was time to fulfill my duties. As the escort I did not really have any responsibilities, but it was an official function. Plus, I wanted to be there to offer support to the Hydes. I would also be able to see mutual friends and acquaintances of Dan and mine, and together we could somewhat ease our collective grief. So, it was back up to Modesto and to the funeral home to spend some more time with Dan.

The Hydes decided to keep Dan's public visitation closed casket even though he was deemed "viewable" at the last minute. The three of them preferred that family and friends remember Dan's busy and fulfilled way of *living*, rather than lying there looking "made up" in a cold, hard box.

The visitation was another exhausting ordeal, but for different reasons. As an introvert, human interaction takes its toll, and participating in hours of it while talking about your dead friend takes it to the next level. I will admit, it was nice to see familiar faces and catch up despite the circumstances. There was a lot of chit-chat, "How have you been?" and the like, along with the shared stories of Dan, which did provide a degree of comfort. I also got to spend more time with the Hydes. I remained in near awe of their strength. I was holding it together much better than I was the day I brought Dan home, yet I still found myself being worn down by all the activity and some of the conversations.

The mingling provided me the opportunity to get all the grisly details about Dan's death. Danny Hwang, who was able to make it out to the services, told a captive audience about how Dan died. In addition to being Dan's roommate, Danny was also in the same unit, 2-35 Cacti. He was in Iraq operating at one of the nearby bases when Dan was killed, and by being in the same unit, he was privy to all the details. Having deployed myself, it is not hard to get the details of what happened in your unit if you put the work in to find out. There were several of us huddled around wanting to hear. Weird to think how we all *wanted* to know how it happened. The information wouldn't bring Dan back, but maybe by knowing it would bring closure of sorts. The unknown has a funny way of making things worse.

I was stoic as Danny recounted the play-by-play of Dan's death. Others were not. The way Danny described it, Dan died a pretty horrible death. Shitty… The crazy thing is that Dan didn't immediately die. The dude was so strong, such a beast, that he stayed alive for enough time to be MEDEVAC'd and for the combat surgeon to have had a chance to operate on him even though his injuries seemed to have condemned him. I wonder if he was in pain? If he knew that he was going to die? What even goes through your mind when you've sustained such horrific injuries? I hope he wasn't in pain. I hope he was at peace and that things just went black after molten metal severed his limbs and pierced his chest cavity.

Knowing the details of Dan's death did not really change anything for me. I was still numb and emotionally exhausted, but it was more a result of the weight I was feeling with the whole situation that had begun almost a week prior. My dead friend was in the other room and here I was serving in an official capacity because of it, all while feeling pressure to flawlessly execute my duties, which were unclear at least during this part of the journey. The Hydes were obviously busy greeting and talking to everyone who came to pay their respects and did not have much for me to do. Restless with my idleness, I wished there was more I could do for them.

There were certainly others struggling with the experience that, in retrospect, I probably could have lent more emotional support. I just did not have it in me to try and console anyone else. I was tired and exhausted and sad and angry and all the emotions. Plus, there wasn't a deep connection like I made with the Hydes when I stepped off the plane. Maybe I was expecting too much of myself. Despite being a social event, the visitation was still very much an event for each individual to deal with in their own way. It was everyone's last chance to "see" Dan before burying him.

DAY 8: FUNERAL

Next to bringing Dan home to his family, the funeral was the hardest day for me. Unlike the previous day, I had more to do as the escort than be on standby and make small talk. Once again, I would be the one to accompany Dan to his next destination, which this time was the final one. I donned my Army Greens again and got back into the head space I experienced back at Dover: I was on duty, and I had a mission to accomplish. My mood was definitely more somber and a small part of me did not want to be there, but I had to see things through.

When I arrived at the funeral home, everyone seemed to be in a similar mood. The Hydes were there, appearing a little more worn down than the previous day, as was Major Soumoy who was synchronizing the final details of the funeral. There was this looming finality I think we were all feeling. Sure, Dan was gone, just not gone-gone like he would be once he was put in the ground. We spent a few more moments with Dan, conducted a final-conditions check for the sequence of events, and then watched Dan get loaded up into the back of the hearse. The Hydes entered their vehicle as part of the funeral procession, which included local Patriot Riders on motorcycles, and I entered the hearse by myself to escort Dan to his final resting place. Once again it was just Dan and I traveling in silence.

The funeral procession took us through all of Modesto, at least it seemed that way. It was a way for the entire community to pay their respects and to bid a final farewell to one of the greatest individuals to have come out of that town. We drove past Dan's neighborhood and past his old high school, Downey High. Lined up outside the school were students, teachers, and supporters, some holdings signs, and

American flags. There were also large banners and signs attached to the school's chain link fence celebrating its newest legend. After the school, we drove up a major avenue towards the cemetery. We drove under several overpasses with supporters, flags, and signs standing by to pay their respects. Like Fresno, Modesto is an afterthought compared to the major cities of California like Los Angeles or San Francisco, but in that moment the place felt a little more important. You had to wonder how many small towns and insignificant cities experienced similar boosts because of some bright star's untimely death.

With Dan behind me, and the outpouring of support I viewed through the hearse window, my emotions stirred again, much like they had when I was about to land in Modesto on Kalitta 1299. I felt the weight of Dan's death, the gravity of my duties, the disbelief that Dan was really gone, the simultaneous love and pain of an entire community, and the weird detachment from the remains resting just behind me. I choked up during some parts of the ride, and during other stretches, I lightly wept. My experience as the escort was coming to its conclusion and all the grief remained. It didn't matter though. I had one more job to do, which was to hand Dan off to the military pallbearers. Our journey together was almost over.

We entered the cemetery, looped around the narrow road past a sea of tombstones and markers, and parked in front of the site where many had already gathered. This was it. I put on my serious Army face as best I could and exited the vehicle. Outside waiting were the pallbearers from the California National Guard to take over for escort duties. I lined the path where they would walk Dan to his grave site and prepared to render honors. Across the way I saw my dad who drove up for the funeral and probably to check on me. I watched as the honor guard unloaded the flag-draped casket. Seeing it this time was much different than when I first saw it at Dover. I wanted to cry out, but I held it together, barely. The pallbearers lifted the casket and slowly trekked to the site. Keeping tears down, I rendered a crisp salute to my dear friend.

With my duties complete, I walked up to my assigned seat in the front row to sit next to the Hydes and the other VIPs – a perk of serving as the escort. Front and center was Dan, and standing off to the side was Brigadier General Patrick Finnegan who was Dan's and my Dean at West Point. We waited there silently as the crowd got in their seats or moved closer, and the official party got in position for their part in the funeral. From Hawaii to Dover to Modesto, nearly 8,000 miles of travel for me, it was time to bury Dan.

The service started and within maybe a minute, I absolutely lost it and began sobbing uncontrollably. It was all too much for me. In my grief, I couldn't help but feel slightly embarrassed due to my complete lack of composure. There were the Hydes sitting next to me, mostly holding it together relatively speaking, and there I was crying like a baby.

I continued sobbing as General Finnegan gave his speech. Despite his senior rank, it was like having a mutual friend talking about Dan and our experiences together at West Point. At one point he made a quip that Dan was such an amazing person that he could turn water into Miller Lite, a joke I had started as a not-so-subtle way to imply that Dan was a Christ-like figure. While the comment garnered a few chuckles, and it was admittedly nice to have a joke of mine make it into the service, it cut into my grief. I kept sobbing. Glenda tried to comfort me, even acknowledging that my joke made it into the service (which I told her at some point during the week), but it did little to calm me. I felt guilty that I was the one being comforted and not the other way around. I really wanted to be the stronger one in the moment, and I wasn't.

At one point, General Finnegan's papers blew off the podium. I was still crying and useless in the moment, and Glenda got out of her seat to pick them up. Feeling bad, I came too and began helping with the papers, along with someone else, to relieve Glenda who should have never gotten out of her seat. Again, there was the contrast between us. Glenda had the sense to do what needed to be done, and the escort overcome with grief could barely do anything. I managed to calm down somewhat as the service continued, sitting there in this sad trance, ready to break down again.

More words were said, and we finally made it to the hardest part of the service, the playing of "Taps." The playing of those notes will break the toughest of soldiers. There's something about the finality of those notes that informs all those listening that it really is over – your comrade is never coming back. Considering my demeanor prior, the playing of the bugle did not affect me as profoundly as perhaps it had others. I was spent. After the playing of "Taps," there was a flyover that Major Soumoy had set up as part of the service. Out on the horizon, the jets flew through the air to honor my friend just as they would do to whip a crowd up with some patriotic posturing prior to a sporting event. With solemn faces we watched in silence.

The service was over and there I was staring at Dan, or his casket rather, once again. I was composed, barely, as the guests began departing, and I got out of my seat to meander through the crowd, not sure of what to do or where to go. Before I left the first row, I ran into General Finnegan. We conversed briefly about West Point and how I knew Dan. I brought up that I was the escort and he reached into his pocket to give me the Dean's challenge coin for my efforts. Funny how it took bringing my dead friend home to his family to finally get one of those from a general serving at West Point.

After my conversation with the Dean, I saw my dad and walked straight to him for a hug that only a parent could give their child. Upon our embrace, I broke down again, still overcome with grief. I wept there in my father's arms until I wasn't anymore. There would be more tears, but it would be my last big cry of the week. The crowd thinned out until all that remained was a small group to say a private farewell to Dan.

We gathered around Dan for the last time with the Hydes. There was a cooler of Coronas waiting there, Dan's favorite beer, and Glenda started handing them out to the remaining group. I've never been a fan of Corona, but I took one when Glenda handed it to me. We all sat there, drinking beer, and having light conversation as the funeral team prepared to lower Dan into the ground. Despite our time in Dan's physical presence coming to an end, the mood was much lighter than it had been during the service. At one point, Dan's Army friends began taking things off their uniforms to place on Dan's casket. Many of them offered up their Ranger Tabs. Not being one do be like everyone else, I ripped off my 25th Infantry Division combat patch and gave it to Dan. Finishing our Coronas, we all stood up and gathered around. It was time. In silence we said our last goodbyes and they lowered him down. And that was that. Dan was secure in his final resting place.

We went back to the Hyde's house for a reception. It was a much lighter affair than the service and a nice reprieve from the previous emotional beat down. I caught up with some of the friends and classmates I avoided at the visitation, and even did some people-watching. It was interesting to see how people handled things post-funeral service. By and large, most in the group seemed to be in a good mood, relatively speaking. Some even seemed to be getting "closer" after the whole experience. I was still a bit shell-shocked, but I wasn't sobbing or crying anymore, and I even traded jokes with Andrea. After everything, it was nice.

That evening the younger crowd let loose and went out to a local bar in Modesto to get drinks and unwind after a rough day. I'm not sure what Dan would think about us going out after his burial, but I know I would want my friends and loved ones to go out and have a good time after burying me. I'm sure Dan would agree. No need to bawl your eyes out the entire time.

During our night out, Andrea would come to call the place "Stab Bar" since someone was stabbed there right before I arrived. I found the name funny, and it made me appreciate Andrea more. She was more like me than her brother was. She was snarky, a tad cynical, profane at times, and was laid back in a sense that she did not take things, or herself, too seriously. She was much stronger than me in the way she handled Dan's death, but I could sense the deep pain she was experiencing, nonetheless. Her brother, her best friend was gone, and I can't imagine the extent of what she was feeling. Still, she handled herself with this powerful grace that was beyond admirable, just like her mother. At one point in the evening Andrea told me that I was her favorite. Taken aback a little bit, I acknowledged my elevated position and told her that I was here for her as I said when I first landed in Modesto. We were close now, tight, bonded by our shared trauma over Dan's death.

We finished up the night at Stab Bar and made our way back home. It was a nice time. We drank and talked and laughed and seemingly enjoyed ourselves, which was a welcome change from everything we had gone through. It was the first event during the week that wasn't about Dan. Not to say that he wasn't in our thoughts, it's just that he wasn't the focus, which I think allowed us to unburden ourselves from our grief for a change. At least that's how I felt, tipsy as I was.

The next day would be Dan's celebration of life. It would be a nice change of pace seeing how death seemed to be the dominant force over the past week. The time had come, and I was ready to finish my journey with Dan.

DAY 9: CELEBRATION OF LIFE

In the morning, we came together at a Baptist church in Modesto to collectively honor Dan one last time. After all the sorrow, it was a nice way to wrap things up, celebrating the man who had brought us all together. For this event, I had no official duties outside of escorting a retired general who was the senior representative for the 2-35 Infantry Cacti Association. It was a much simpler task, and I did not mind at all that I wasn't there to eulogize or do something equally visible. I was largely there as a spectator, like the many others who had come to celebrate. As part of the official party, the general and I got priority seating near the front. Waiting for things to get started, we engaged in some small talk about our military service. He asked why I did not have a combat patch and I explained that I ripped it off and put it on Dan's casket. He seemed to be okay with this being the reason my uniform was not exactly at it should have been.

As I sat there, it dawned on me that this was my first time being in church since I went to church that Sunday morning with Dan in Hawaii right before he deployed. I did not want to be there, but Dan ended up making me comfortable, even glad to have attended. "I'm glad you're here," he told me. It meant a lot in the moment. Fast forward five months and Dan Hyde had me right back in church contemplating religion and faith and what it all meant. I wonder if he intended it that way. At any rate, it was another full circle event involving me and Dan. Fate perhaps, or maybe I was looking too much into things.

Still deep in thought, the celebration began. Kicking off the event with opening remarks was Andrea. She gave an amazing speech; heartfelt, humorous, and something only a sibling could deliver. She was so poised during the entire thing, hardly even a crack in her voice as she eulogized her brother to help all of us come to terms with his loss. I probably would've come to pieces after the first sentence or two, but she held it together, displaying the strength and liveliness we needed to see during a celebration rather than a memorial. She set the right tone.

Following Andrea, were eulogies from Dan's uncle, a pastor in North Dakota, his minister, his childhood karate instructor, his close friend Derek, his basketball coach, and Danny Hwang. The speeches were all fantastic, each one providing additional insights into a friend I would never fully know.

While hearing all the great things about Dan, I couldn't help but think of what people would say about me if I was the one who had been killed. What would my funeral look like? How many people would show up? Who would eulogize me? How would my mom take it? My dad? My brothers? Did I matter to the extent that Dan did to all these people? How would I be remembered? Was it normal to think about these things at someone else's service? A lot of difficult questions crossed my mind as I sat there imagining my own funeral and celebration of life.

Focusing back on Dan's service, with the eulogies complete, the event transitioned to a video montage with accompanying music. The video gave us a sense of who Dan was, though it was largely absent of the life and vitality that we had lost with the actual person. Pictures can't do a full life justice; however, it was nice to see Dan being Dan, living his life before it was cut short.

During the video, the song "I'll Be Missing You," by Puff Daddy, played. Glenda had been asked by Dan to play that particular song, should anything ever happen to him. I was never a fan of the song since it came out in 1997, but I enjoyed it for the first time in my life as photos of Dan, my friend, flashed across the screen. It was so Dan Hyde. I always found it funny that he was this strait-laced white kid who loved rap more than any other genre of music. I probably asked him why at some point, but never got deep enough into it to remember or understand.

Another song that played during the video was "Daniel" by Elton John. This song stirred my emotions more than anything else had during the service. The lyrics spoke to the situation we were all in. We were saying goodbye to Daniel, a star in every aspect. The melancholy notes of the melody meshed with the vocals and captured everything I had felt over the week: *Oh, I miss Daniel, oh, I miss him so much; Daniel, my brother . . . do you still feel the pain; I can see Daniel waving goodbye; Oh God it looks like Daniel must be the clouds in my eyes.* Hard as it was to hear, it was perfect.

Shortly after the video, the celebration of life concluded and my time as the escort drew to a close. The crowd lingered in the church for a bit, with some making their way to pay their respects and others mingling in and around the pews. Not wanting to stand there awkwardly, I thanked and departed ways with the general and made my way outside to say my final goodbyes to my friends, classmates, and new acquaintances, and to say goodbye to the new family I found in the Hydes.

The goodbye to Brian, Glenda, and Andrea was a much lighter affair than the hello we had had five days earlier, which at this point seemed like an eternity ago. There were smiles and laughing and we discussed getting together in the future, as dear friends do. There was also a profound gratefulness there between us that went without saying. Virtual strangers a week ago, we were now bonded by the experience. Having all lost something irreplaceable in Dan, we had something with each other now that made our lives just a little bit fuller than they had been on March 7th.

And like that it was over. For over a week I had dedicated myself to Dan Hyde, along with so many others. We celebrated him. We honored him. We mourned him. Damn near worshiped him. But he was gone. It was now on us to go back to our lives and a new normal where Dan Hyde was dead, killed in action during the Iraq War. Life goes on whether or not we decide to go on along with it.

What to make of it all? Where do we go from here? My experience as Dan's escort was transformational. But to what extent? I'm not sure I'll ever truly know. What I do know is that I'm glad I was able to be there for my friend, and more importantly, for his family, as painful as it was. I wouldn't have it any other way. I also know that tragedy can lead to new beginnings, the whole "darkest before the dawn" if you will. I have the Hyde family in my life now and a refined outlook on what life entails.

Life is precious and fleeting, and it's on each individual to make the most of it despite the insurmountable amount of shit it can throw at you. "Do not accept mediocrity in any aspect of your life," as Dan had been saying since he was in high school. At such a young age Dan had already figured it out, like some sage in a young man's body. Maybe that's why he's gone. He had nothing left to prove.

And in all actuality perhaps gone is the wrong word to use. Sure, Dan is no longer physically with us; the vessel is in the ground. His spirit on the other hand is very much alive. In fact, after everything I witnessed this past week, his spirit is thriving. Dan's life was a true blessing, but his death was a sort of blessing in its own right because it challenged us all to be better versions of ourselves. Dan will live on through me and through the many others that he touched during his short, but full, life. That is his legacy, and it is a legacy I will do my damnedest to uphold until the end of my days knowing full well I'll never be Dan Hyde. I think he would be good with that. It would be enough for him to smirk and tell me, "I'm glad you're here."

ADJUSTING

I remember wandering the halls of Thomas Downey High School just over two weeks after learning of my son's tragic death in Iraq. I was back to work as a paraprofessional at the high school he, his sister, and I all attended.

In the months and years that followed Daniel's death on March 7, 2009, there have been speeches, plaques, recognitions, tournaments, seminars, awards, ceremonies, even a statue, honoring him. Military men and women have competed in races and events they felt were challenging and appropriate to the level of athleticism that Daniel had demonstrated. Tee shirts and dog tags bore his football number (13) and his quote, "Do not accept mediocrity in any aspect of your life." Or for short, "No mediocrity." This quote was Daniel's response to an interview question at the end of his senior year of high school. The local paper featured outstanding high school students that were continuing their education. Daniel had been asked during the interview, "What advice would you offer to teenagers?" This quote was his response.

A bronze statue was designed and placed at his beloved Thomas Downey High School so that students could learn of the hometown hero who had walked the very halls they were walking.

The years pass but the pain does not.

One year and then another and another…

1LT DANIEL HYDE MEMORIAL SCHOLARSHIP

Thomas Downey High School

Immediately and generously after Daniel's death, money began to pour into the high school. People want to help and do not know what else to do. Money is often the outcome of that thoughtfulness. As checks arrived, I imagine there was a strong desire to formulate a plan. I say I imagine because I have no idea or recollection how this scholarship started, who was instrumental in it, or how it progressed so quickly. When I asked the principal 12 years after the first scholarship was awarded, he modestly said he was not sure. However, I am sure he was instrumental in leading the endeavor. While communicating with him one comment resonated, "There were so many staff members and community members who loved Daniel, and loved your family, and they wanted to help."

It reminded me how incredibly grateful I was that whatever I requested was accomplished. Everything except for pulling weeds in my backyard. When people would ask what they could do I would say, "We are going to gather in our backyard after the service on Friday and the weeds really need to be pulled." No one took me up on that request. I laugh now thinking about this. But seriously EVERY OTHER JOB was done. I would say it out loud and someone would take care of it.

I probably didn't thank everyone I needed to at that time, so I will now. If you had anything to do with helping our family IN ANY WAY after Daniel died, we are humbly and sincerely grateful! We could never have survived without the help of friends and family and the overwhelming support and love from the community, Daniel's village, which continues steadfast, years later.

Within days, the plan to create a scholarship to benefit other students seemed to be one obvious choice. Therefore, every year starting in 2009, Thomas Downey High School has presented a financial award to one outstanding student who plans to continue their education.

As of 2022, over $18,000.00 has been awarded to deserving students committed to "making a difference" as they work to carry on Daniel's goal of "no mediocrity."

It is hard for me to believe that the first recipient of the 1LT Daniel Hyde Memorial Scholarship was awarded $1,500.00 in 2009, just a couple of months after Daniel's death. I remember being at the event. I remember speaking about Daniel, the scholarship, and saying the name of the young lady who received it. However, any recollection about how said scholarship came to be *that quickly* is lost on me.

Lauren (Daniels) Wilson was the first recipient of the 1LT Daniel Hyde Scholarship in 2009. During high school, Lauren was involved in yearbook, cheerleading (I was her coach), and track. She was class President her senior year. After high school Lauren attended UC Santa Barbara where she received a BA in Communications with a minor in Art History. Her first job out of college was with the Santa Barbara Zoo where she managed all their photography and marketing platforms. She enjoyed this job, which used both her communication degree and her love of photography. Lauren currently resides in San Diego and works in Commercial Real Estate. She enjoys her job as well as her additional roles as a wife and mother.

Megan Carley was the 2011 recipient. I coached Megan in cheerleading as well. Megan still says today that cheer was her favorite activity during high school. Megan's mom Laurie and I have become close since Daniel's death. Laurie is one of my many gifts of friendship from my sweet boy as a result of his untimely departure. Megan attended UC Berkeley and majored in Business Administration. She currently is employed with Salesforce working in sales strategy. She helps sales executives with strategic planning and provides operational support to help them run their business successfully. Prior to her current job, she worked as a healthcare consultant helping hospitals and health care systems recover lost revenue from insurance companies.

In 2013, there were two amazing candidates, so the scholarship panel asked that we award both outstanding students: Sierra Durham and Spencer Garrett.

Sierra attended Cal Poly San Luis Obispo and majored in Chemistry. She graduated *summa cum laude* and in 2021 was working on her PhD at UC Davis in Food Science. Sierra researched oligosaccharides in milk. These are sugars that are bigger than lactose and promote good gut health especially for babies. These compounds are in breast milk but not infant formula. Sierra's goal is to find another natural source that could be used in formula to provide formula-fed babies with more of the benefits of breast milk. In the summer of 2021 Sierra interned at Gallo Winery in Modesto, CA.

Spencer attended UC Berkeley and double majored in Bioengineering and Linguistics with a minor in Conservation and Resource Studies. After graduating, Spencer did an AmeriCorps program through Notre Dame Mission Volunteers (not affiliated with the university, just sharing the same name) called Seton Teaching Fellows, where he taught kindergarten in the South Bronx. Spencer is currently teaching fifth grade at a Catholic school in East Harlem and will continue there while completing his masters. After completion of his masters at Notre Dame, Spencer hopes to work in Catholic Education Administration as either a dean or principal. Eventually, Spencer would like to transition into developing education policy with particular interest in serving students and families in low-income communities.

2017 brought an emotional full circle love story. A former student of Sonoma Elementary School, where Daniel and his sister Andrea attended, recalled bringing in items to send to Daniel in Iraq and writing to Daniel in 2009. A few years later, as a high school senior, he was awarded the scholarship after relaying this beautiful story in his qualifying essay. Brandon Madrigal, the 2017 recipient of the

1LT Daniel Hyde Scholarship, attended Stanislaus State and majored in Marketing. Brandon relayed his love to our family for giving him the chance to attend Stanislaus State and reach new goals.

Our family would love to see this scholarship continue at Thomas Downey High School so that for years to come, young people will continue to be recognized and awarded for their academic efforts and be assisted financially. Thus, allowing them to find their way into the future, making a difference with no mediocrity!

DARRIN

I met Daniel Hyde at Sonoma Elementary school.

Daniel and I played baseball together on the Sonoma Dolphins baseball team.

We were separated in junior high and high school, attending different schools and we did not see one another for years.

One night after a high school football game, I ran into Daniel, and we chatted for a few minutes. I felt like no time had passed. On that memorable night I realized how accomplished Daniel had been. Even as early as elementary school he was a talented shortstop and a great teammate.

I remember Daniel missing school one Friday back in the sixth grade and our teacher, Mr. Wierschem, announcing that Daniel was going to be testing to receive his black belt in tae kwon do. I was amazed at that. I did not know anyone else who had accomplished earning a black belt.

Even though Daniel was a great athlete at such a young age, the thing that I really loved was the way Daniel treated people.

That night after the high school football game was the last time I ever spoke to Daniel, but I never forgot him.

When my wife Christina and I had our little boy in 2012, three years after Daniel died in Iraq, I told Christina I would like to name our son Daniel, after my elementary school friend. I realized that by naming our son Daniel I would have a lifelong reminder of my good friend and that our son Daniel would receive a name that had special meaning. Our son would grow up to know who Daniel Hyde was and would also learn how Daniel treated others.

DANIEL JOHN RUBALCAVA was born on July 7, 2012, in Modesto, CA, to Darrin and Christina Rubalcava.

MOVING

On a warm summer day in 2013, while I was working out in the front yard of our California home, Brian asked me if I would consider moving to Las Vegas. My response was automatically NO. Brian had asked this ridiculous question before and it resulted in the same fast answer. However, for some reason, on this particular day Brian persisted. Finally feeling guilty I asked him why?

Brian works for a charitable foundation through the Lutheran Church. His work takes him to several different locations. At the time he was contracted with a church in Las Vegas, NV. He had been traveling to Las Vegas once a month for a year or so.

We were still reeling from Daniel's death. We both worked full time and tried to merely survive on a day-to-day basis.

Brian was growing to love Las Vegas and had been interested in getting out of California for quite some time. Modesto was basically the only home I had ever known and moving seemed impossible for me. Leaving Daniel's grave was at the top of the list of reasons why I could not go. It felt as though I would be abandoning Daniel, and I was not about to do that. Brian had concrete reasons to move, but I still could not fathom leaving the friends we had acquired over a 40-year span. We both had family in Modesto as well as in Sacramento and Fremont. We had lived in the same house for over 30 years. There was so much history for both of us in Modesto.

As Brian persisted, I began doing some research. I began to say it out loud to close friends. "Brian wants to drag me to Las Vegas to LIVE." Brian continued to talk to me about the positives for moving. He was killing himself commuting one hour each way every day to Livermore to his office. Sometimes that one hour could turn into 90-minutes. He had a 90-minute drive from our home each time he flew out to Las Vegas or any other traveling destination for work. Moving would cut his commute time down considerably since the Las Vegas airport is just 30 minutes from everywhere we would live. *PERHAPS* Andrea, our only remaining child would enjoy coming to visit in Las Vegas instead of Modesto. Andrea was living in Southern California and the commute was about the same to either location.

Brian loved Nevada for its crystal-clear blue skies, the mountains, the southern landscape, and the weather.

As Brian continued to talk about Nevada and all the possibilities, I listened more carefully.

JENNIFER

Memories are tricky. I've tried so hard to remember the first time I met Dan Hyde but can't. Dan and I were classmates at West Point, and we most likely met during our Yearling (sophomore) year, but became better friends during our Cow (junior) year when I started hanging out with Nick (my husband) and his brother, Matt.

Dan was close with Nick and Matt and on long weekends, he'd join them at their house in Massachusetts since flying home to California was difficult. Typical visits to the Barry's house included yard work in the mornings followed by movies and card games in the evening. Dan was a regular at the Barry's home, so much so that we'd call it his "East Coast" home.

During one visit, we were all seated around the dinner table while Mrs. Barry served dessert - brownies with whipped cream. I clearly remember everyone taking a brownie and passing the whipped cream can around after putting a big dollop of whipped cream on their brownie. Everyone that is except for Dan. Dan, ever so carefully put an even layer of whipped cream on top so each bite had the same amount.

It was no surprise when Dan was selected for a senior leadership position our Firstie (senior) year at West Point. We graduated on May 26, 2007, and a week later, Dan was a groomsman in my wedding to Nick Barry.

At the rehearsal dinner, Dan spoke and gave me a shirt with a picture of a bride and groom with the words "Big Mistake" written at the bottom. When Dan held up the shirt, everyone saw that he crossed out "Big Mistake" and replaced it with "Great Idea," which made the entire room erupt in laughter.

And that was Dan. Through his actions, he stood out from everyone else around him. It did not matter if we were at the dinner table, in a classroom, or in the field completing Army training. Dan was special. He always tried his best and gave everything 100%. If he failed, which didn't happen often, he picked himself up and tried again. He was also the first person to stop what he was doing to help someone else. He was caring, hardworking, determined, and humble. He was the best of the best.

My wedding was the last time I saw Dan in person. He was killed in Samarra, Iraq, on March 7, 2009. He gave his life to our country and died a hero.

In the relatively short amount of time Nick and I knew Dan, he made a lasting impact. So much so, that when we found out we were expecting a son, in August of 2013, we wanted him to have Dan's name as his middle name.

Caden Daniel made a dramatic entrance into the world on August 22, 2013. I know Dan was watching over us and our team of doctors that day. Dan always took care of those around him when he was alive, and I know he continues to take care of his family and friends from heaven.

Dan was a wonderful friend and a true hero.

NICK

I met Dan in the fall of 2005. It was in late August, the start of reorganization week my Firstie (senior) year at West Point. My roommate and I had returned a day early from a brief leave period after our summer training. We were moving everything we owned halfway across the cadet area to our new home in Eisenhower barracks. Since we were assigned to the Brigade Staff, we were asked to come back a day before the rest of the Corps. There were very few people around to watch us struggle back and forth in the late August humidity. At some point early in the process, Dan showed up outside of our door and offered us the use of a laundry cart he had somehow acquired. I cannot understate the magnitude of this gesture, it saved us hours of work. This was the kind of person Dan was: He would go out of his way to help two complete strangers. We got to talking and I could tell right away that he was an impressive individual. Neither Dan nor I knew too many people on the newly-formed staff, so we started hanging out together.

Dan had a focus and a purpose that would be downright intimidating if he wasn't such a nice guy. I considered myself focused but found that Dan took it to a higher level. I had no doubt he would take on a senior leadership role in the Corps, the following year.

The year we met, Dan had an unbelievably difficult job on the Brigade Staff. He was the First Sergeant. He was *the only* junior member of the staff, responsible for discipline, accountability, and basically making the senior staff do whatever the Tactical Officer wanted us to do, but we did not do. Many would have struggled in this role, surrounded by those with higher rank, some of whom are the top performers in their class. Yet, no one messed with Dan or gave him a hard time. I never heard him raise his voice or argue with anyone. Everyone who met or worked with him respected him and recognized that he had the qualities of a great leader. We became fast friends. Within a few weeks he was cutting my hair in my barracks room.

Yes, of course he had the talent to cut his own hair too, something which I would have never attempted. My brother, Matt, a Yearling at the time, spent a lot of time over at my room hanging out and getting away from the routine of his own company. We both really enjoyed spending time with Dan. Matt and Dan would commiserate over their love of gangster Rap, something which I never understood. Being from California, Dan found it difficult to escape for four-day weekends or other short breaks. So, we invited him to our house which was only a few hours' drive from the academy. This thrilled my father, as he quickly discovered that the three of us, Dan, my brother Matt, and myself, could move large rocks and other heavy things around their property. Dan helped move one large boulder that had bothered my dad for years. Today, it is still where Dan moved it. We soon had him splitting firewood, walking in the hills, and playing hockey on frozen ponds.

Years later, I returned to West Point as an instructor in the Department of Electrical Engineering and Computer Science. By this time, the academy had created the Dan Hyde challenge, an arduous physical challenge completed during cadet summer training. I taught mostly Firsties, who often surprised me by discussing Dan or the challenge at some point during our time together. At the end of the first semester, of each of the three years I was there, I would take some time from a lesson to talk about Dan. I explained to my students that they need to take time to appreciate the tremendous people around them. I told them to always take the time to enjoy each other's company, learn from one another, and help each other out. The world is a dangerous place and this profession, even more so. I would tell my students to cherish every moment with each other because you never know when you will run out of those moments.

Caden, this is the reason your middle name is Daniel. It was important to your mom and me that you know Dan's story. We know you are beginning to be old enough to understand.

We are glad you know Dan was a hero who died fighting in a war. We are glad you know Dan was a dear friend to our entire family.

CADEN DANIEL BARRY was born on August 22, 2013, at Fort Hood, TX, to Nicholas and Jennifer (MacGibbon) Barry.

JERALYN

I grew up on Tallent Drive in Modesto, California. My family lived across the street from Daniel Hyde's grandparents, who lived next door to a martial arts school that began in the garage of Rick and Annabelle Jones. I was one of Rick's first class of students.

Ernie Reyes is THE Grand Master of the entire World West Coast Martial Arts Association. Through the system, as you progress in belt ranking and become an advanced student, you are encouraged to teach and give value to the lower belt students. I was one of Daniel Hyde's instructors during his early days of training. I began teaching when I was 15 years old and started with the youngest students. Daniel was just beginning his martial arts journey at seven years old.

Daniel was a strong student from the start. I had always wanted to enter the field of education and had a great deal of experience with young children, even though I was only 15 years old. I saw something in Daniel at seven years old and in the years following as we both progressed through the ranks. He never gave up and pushed himself in a way that I rarely saw in children his age. He was very respectful to me and all his instructors. Daniel was capable in so many ways; he was intelligent, athletic, friendly, and kind.

After high school, I moved to Michigan to attend Calvin College. Eventually I married and we stayed here in Michigan. Often, when I called home and talked to my parents, they would give me updates on the neighbors and the neighborhood. Sometimes during conversation my parents would tell me something about Daniel that they had heard from his grandparents. For instance: I knew he was a successful football player in high school, I knew he joined the military, and I knew that he was sent to the war. I also was told about his death very soon after it happened because of my parent's connections to people in the neighborhood. Daniel's grandparents or someone from the Jones' family told my parents that Daniel had been killed in Iraq.

Through the power of social media, I was reconnected to Daniel's parents after Daniel's death. I read the stories that Daniel's mom shared about him, and I saw pictures and heard testimonies about the impact he had on the people around him.

In 2013 when my husband and I were expecting our third son, we were struggling to agree on a name. We had already named two boys and this time we did not seem to be able to come to a consensus. I suggested the name Daniel and at first my husband, Ben, was not sure, but finally he consented if the baby's middle name could be Benjamin. I also had to keep the baby's name a secret until after he or she was born, so we called the baby, Benji. I wanted to name our baby boy Daniel because I liked the name, and I loved the character of Daniel from the Bible. In addition, I remembered my former martial arts student that I had taught years earlier. I thought about the stories I had heard from my parents about his life choices and the sacrifice he made. I knew about Daniel Hyde's upbringing, and after his death, I became more and more aware of the life he had lived. I saw him as a God-honoring young man with great integrity. Daniel seemed to be exactly the kind of person I would love to see my son become and we decided that Daniel Benjamin was a perfect name for our baby, number three. Later I also realized the significance of the number 13 in Daniel Hyde's life. My prayer for our son, Daniel, is that he become a man that follows closely after God, lives with integrity, and offers respect to all those he encounters, much like the boy I once knew all those years ago.

DANIEL BENJAMIN BELOTE was born on October 7, 2013, in Climax, MI, to Ben and Jeralyn (DeVries) Belote.

Baby Daniel Belote makes three namesakes, and 2013 was ending as a remarkably memorable year!

13

The number 13 has a significant presence in our lives.

Daniel wore the number 13 all four years that he played high school football. He chose the number because his dad wore the number 13 for baseball when he was growing up. Daniel's number and jersey were retired on September 11, 2009, from the Thomas Downey High School football program six months after his death in Iraq.

When we moved to our first home in Las Vegas there were 13 steps from the landing to the second floor. I may have not noticed that one, but Brian pointed it out. We went to a lot of shows having just moved to Las Vegas and randomly our tickets would direct us to seat 13. We had gone to a 49er game a few years after Daniel's death (he LOVED the 49ers) and one of the three of us: myself, my husband, or our daughter, had seat number 13. In airplanes, hotel rooms, offices, and so many other places we see the number.

I notice number 13 so routinely I hardly blink anymore. Do I think it is "just a coincidence"? I do not. When I see 13, I am reminded of a brave young quarterback taking hit after hit, and always returning to the huddle encouraging his team they could still win. They would be down by 20 points, but Daniel never gave up on the win.

Daniel spoke frequently and fondly of his football years. He had never played the game until he entered high school. Though he loved basketball, golf, baseball, and martial arts, no other sport affected him the way football did: The experience, the hardships, the camaraderie, the exhausting practices with an incredibly small team all four years (most of the team played both offense and defense) the agony of defeat, the BROTHERHOOD. Daniel referred to his football years with great reverence.

With such great love of the sport in general and Daniel's personal football experiences I find it comforting that his football number appears before us repeatedly. It keeps us connected.

Feeling humbled after being voted Football Homecoming King
at Thomas Downey High School.

"Greater love has no one than this, that he lay down his life for his friends."

John 15:13

Daniel and I grew up together. Our families are so close I'm proud to call him my older brother. My parents were his Godparents and I'm very blessed that his parents are mine. He was the perfect role model for me to look up to as we both grew older. When he was away at West Point, I would look forward to visiting him during his short trips home to hear about his new experiences. Many of these sounded so intense there was no way I could even fathom doing them myself, especially after hearing about the challenges he faced becoming a Ranger.

I vividly remember the last time I saw him. We were both sitting on the couch in his living room watching football and talking about the 49ers and the Giants' upcoming season, but the one thing that profoundly moved me was when I asked him about his deployment. He never once hesitated to answer my questions about it, and not once did he say he was nervous or even hint that he was in the tone of his voice. I knew he was confident in the mission he was about to embark on, and that type of courage is something I have never seen in any other person I've met. Daniel did everything in his life with great vigor and strived for greatness. I know nobody is perfect but if there were any person who came close, that person is Daniel. Maybe that is why our Lord decided it was his time. Maybe our Lord needed a helping hand to watch over this chaotic world and what better a candidate than Daniel. I know in my heart that is the reason why, but it still hurts so bad to know that he's gone for now until we meet again in heaven. God bless all those who have given their lives serving our great nation.

~

Thomas Goodwin
Modesto, California

STILL TAKING CARE OF US

I was coming around to thinking that if Brian and I needed to, we could move to Las Vegas until Brian retired. Then if we wanted, we could move back to Modesto. I was still leery, but Brian had a job that required the move and I needed to be the compromising partner at the time.

In the summer of 2013, I had driven over and stayed with Brian a couple of times during his work weeks in Las Vegas. While I was there, we looked at housing and neighborhoods. Prior to this time my only knowledge of Las Vegas was the strip. I honestly had no concept of "normal" living in Sin City.

I finally agreed to uprooting our long history in Modesto, CA. We found a community in the northwest part of Las Vegas that was just starting to build. This community was located 30 miles north of the strip. In a Las Vegas new build, you choose an area where a new subdivision is being developed and make a small down payment to the builder so construction can begin on your home.

As copies of my newly published book, *24 Years And 40 Days,* arrived at our Modesto home in late October, a friend from high school offered to host my first book signing. It took place on Veterans Day, November 11, 2013. I will always be indebted to Susan and her husband Mike for graciously hosting that memorable evening at H – B Saloon, in Oakdale, CA.

The bronze statue that had been crafted for Daniel was set to be dedicated by Lieutenant General Robert Caslen, Jr. (retired). LTG Caslen knew Daniel at West Point and was deployed with Daniel's unit to Iraq. LTG Caslen was in Iraq when Daniel was killed. He graciously called on a few occasions to check up on us and at the end of one conversation he said, "If there is ever anything I can do for you…". I took him up on his offer and LTG Caslen made plans to come to Modesto. During his time in Modesto, he visited Daniel's grave, dedicated the statue at Thomas Downey High School, and gave a town hall chat in the high school auditorium.

LTG Caslen mentioned in his chat the movie *Saving Private Ryan*. He spoke about the significance of EARNING the freedoms that military heroes grant us in the ultimate sacrifices they make. He said we should all strive to live each day EARNING those sacrifices.

In the afternoon that day as I witnessed this decorated three-star General get down on one knee and weep over my son's grave, I became painfully aware of how stricken he was by the deaths of so many **young** men and women. This is a memory I will not forget.

Our new build in Las Vegas was coming along and it was time to make a sizable down payment. The expected payment was around $40,000.00. Our home in Modesto had not yet sold. We had a back-up plan for obtaining the money, but we did not want to put that plan into action if we could avoid it.

While Brian was at work one day he received an email from a T-Rowe Price representative. The email asked if he knew or was related to Daniel Brian Hyde. Brian responded to the email stating that our son Daniel Brian Hyde had been killed in Iraq four years prior. The T-Rowe Price representative told Brian there was an account with some money in it that would require our attention. Brian asked how much money, but the representative said he could not divulge any information until he had proof of Daniel's death.

When Brian got home that evening, he told me about the email. Immediately I said, "Stop thinking what you are thinking." I knew Brian was looking for that $40,000.00. I said, "There is NO WAY that much money exists in an account undiscovered for four years." I was certain the account had perhaps a couple hundred dollars in it.

I WAS WRONG.

Daniel's T-Rowe Price account had almost EXACTLY the dollar amount we needed to make the FULL down payment on our new Las Vegas home.

Unbelievable! Daniel was still taking care of us four years after his death.

In mid-December of 2013, the movers came and packed up our Modesto home. Brian and I drove to Las Vegas and moved into our new home on December 19, 2013.

ROGER AND ERICA

We met Dan through mutual friends while he was living in Georgia. Dan was spending a year at Fort Benning completing his Officer Training courses including Ranger and Airborne Schools. During that year our paths crossed frequently, and we always enjoyed our time with Dan.

Roger: I first met Dan when he came to town with Danny Hwang and other guys in the Army that spent time partying in Atlanta. Dan and I hit it off right away. I saw he was reserved in his demeanor compared to my rowdy group of friends and Dan's military buddies. I made it my mission to include Dan, to make him feel at home and ensure he would have a great time during his visits. Dan would stay at my place and feel at home since my friends were easy-going, as was my girlfriend at the time, Erica. That is how Erica got to know Dan. She realized that Dan was a genuinely nice guy, and we all enjoyed every opportunity to spend time with Dan. My family is large and as they all got to know Dan, they too welcomed him with open arms.

Dan was smart, polite, and charming to everyone. It was not difficult to see how everyone became attached to him. I became Dan's confidant in conversations that I knew he was not having with others. I respected that trust he put on me. We wrote a lot of letters to one another during Dan's time in Ranger School. I knew it was important to keep his mental health strong and to have a friend write to him, as well as for him to receive correspondence. I have never been so committed to keep up correspondence with any friend, but I knew what this meant to Dan.

Dan was recycled after his first attempt at phase one of Ranger School. I went to retrieve him for a quick break when he finally passed phase one. It had been a long several weeks and he was exhausted.

Glenda called Dan's cell when she thought he would have had time to get home, and I answered his phone. I introduced myself to Glenda and explained that Dan had passed out at his desk while trying to do some computer work. I tried my best to get him to "give up" and go lay down but Dan insisted he had no time for a nap. However, the lack of sleep during two rounds of phase one of Ranger School got the best of "Super Dan" and he dropped face down at his desk. I could not bear to wake him, so I let him sleep right there, just as he had fallen asleep.

Erica: Dan was many things but what I remember the most was how thoughtful he was. On one occasion, I purchased a beautiful new mailbox and it sat around for a long time waiting to be put in place. Roger kept putting off the installation of the mailbox. One day Dan told me he was going to get that mailbox in the ground for me, therefore motivating Roger to help him and get it done. Together Roger and Dan installed my mailbox and to this day every time I go get the mail…I think of Dan. Another great memory I have of him is when he was preparing to leave for Iraq or maybe he was leaving for Ranger training. I can't remember, but it was prior to Mother's Day and Dan made sure to set up a delivery for his mom. Lots of guys (including my husband) hold off until the last moment, but Dan was always so thoughtful and made sure it would be delivered ahead of time.

Roger: When we learned of Dan's death in Iraq, Erica and I made the trip out to California to attend Dan's services and to get to know his family. He had become that important to us.

Erica and I knew we wanted to honor Dan in a significant way. When we had our first son, his name had already been chosen years earlier. We were thrilled to be having a second son and were excited to honor our friend through our son. We kept trying different combinations of names to decide how they would fit together and finally decided Hyde would become a permanent part of our second son's life and would be our second son's middle name.

There were several Dans that we hung out with so the guys would call Dan by his last name, HYDE. We thought that was perfect for our son.

Erica and Roger: Nico has asked many questions about Dan over the years, and we converse about Dan to Nico on a regular basis. We tell Nico what Dan meant to us as a dear friend and the amazing man he was. His leadership, selflessness, and thoughtfulness are some of the many things that made us want to name our son after Dan. We know Nico will hold Dan as an additional guiding light in his life. Nico is already brilliant, yet kind, with the heart of a warrior at the mere age of 8. Dan was an old soul and Nico is turning out to be as well. Both thinkers, and Nico is showing himself to be a leader like Dan. We love the connection they have even though they never met. Dan would be proud…

NICOLAS HYDE TRUEBA was born on January 20, 2014, in Atlanta, GA, to Erica and Roger Trueba.

★

ANNETTE AND JIM

Annette Keller served as the Director of Christian Education and Youth at the church where our kids grew up, Grace Lutheran. Her husband, Jim, was called to be the Preschool and Before-and-after-school-care Director. The two of them moved out to California in 1990 when Daniel was five and Andrea was three.

During their teenage years Daniel and Andrea did not participate in many youth events or activities at the church. Their schedules were jam-packed. However, they were in church every Sunday morning. They encountered Jim and Annette from elementary through high school years, as Sunday School teachers and leaders. Annette recalls a time in Sunday School years ago when she asked the kids if they have someone in their life they can "talk" to, a friend or relative, someone they can always count on. Daniel told her, "I don't need anyone else. I have my mom and dad."

Jim eventually went to Seminary to become a Pastor and currently Jim and Annette serve at a church in Fort Wayne, Indiana. Annette became close friends with a Burmese woman named Hannah. It is customary among the Burmese people to ask a very respected member of the culture and church to choose a baby's first name for the parents. Then the baby is traditionally given an American name as its middle name. When Hannah asked Annette to choose her baby's middle name, Jim and Annette had just finished reading my first book about Daniel's life and death. They decided Daniel would be a perfect middle name. They told Hannah the story of our son Daniel and said they would like Daniel to be her son's middle name.

Our great thanks to Pastor Jim and Annette Keller for introducing our Daniel to the Thait family. When Jordan Daniel was born, I sent the family a copy of my book so that they could get to know our Daniel Hyde.

JORDAN DANIEL THAIT was born on August 11, 2015, in Fort Wayne, IN, to Than and Hannah Thait.

R. J.

While I will never forget him, I do not actually remember the first time I met Daniel Hyde. The lead-up to our deployment was a blur, with long hours and a lot of turnover in personnel that occurs in Army units between deployments. It seemed like someone was always leaving and a new person showing up each day as Alpha Company, 2nd Battalion, 35th Infantry Regiment (or 2-35 for short) geared up for our deployment.

As most of the people who welcomed me to Hawaii headed on to their next assignments, Daniel and several of the other infantry lieutenants began arriving *en masse* prior to our upcoming deployment to Iraq.

Even though Daniel was not initially assigned to Alpha Company, I had gotten to know him through the officer workouts and other events that 2-35 organized to help us get to know one another. However, my friendship with Daniel took root when Danny Hwang, one of the Infantry platoon leaders in Alpha Company, suggested that the three of us rent a penthouse for the last few weeks before we deployed to Iraq. Danny pointed out that we all would need somewhere to stay after we broke our leases and put all our stuff in storage. While other officers in our same position found friends, who weren't deploying, to stay with, or rented a modest hotel room, Danny had his eyes set on an incredible 2-bedroom, 2-bathroom penthouse at the Ala Moana Hotel in Waikiki. He then approached Daniel and I to go in with him on it. Danny highlighted the money we would save because there was a full kitchen we could use, while extolling the hotel's amenities and the simple fact that there was no better way to spend our last weeks before Iraq than in a luxurious penthouse. Danny's arguments and persistence were hard to ignore, and Daniel and I quickly signed up.

Danny was rewarded for his efforts with the master bedroom and bath, and Daniel and I shared the second bedroom and bathroom.

Though we were all busy with last-minute training and deployment preparation, the three of us bonded over cooking meals together and hanging out after work. We would watch TV, play Rock Band, and talk about our upcoming deployment, our lives, our families, and what we hoped to do after we all got back. We spent the weekends by the pool during the day and hosting parties at night before venturing out to explore Waikiki. We would attend Danny's church each Sunday to clear our heads and prepare our hearts for the upcoming week. When it came time to leave for Iraq we were relaxed, rested, and felt we were ready.

Fast forward a few months. Danny left Alpha Company taking a more senior position in a different company, still in 2-35 but on a bigger Forward Operating Base (FOB) – FOB Brassfield-Mora. Daniel joined Alpha Company as one of our platoon leaders. While most of 2-35 was stationed at FOB Brassfield-Mora, Alpha Company was stationed out of a small patrol base - Patrol Base Olson - in the heart of Samarra, 120-strong in a city of nearly 350,000 Iraqis. Given the isolated nature of our location and the close quarters in which we lived, the men of Alpha Company were a tight group, and the six officers, even tighter. The friendship Daniel and I formed in Hawaii grew stronger in this setting, as we worked side by side trying to make a difference in our corner of the war. We talked continually about the stress and challenges we faced along the way.

Just as my friendship with Daniel started without much fanfare, the day I lost Daniel started out in a similar fashion. I was on my way down to the command center early on the morning of March 7. I had to cut through where the cardio equipment was located to get there. I noticed Daniel working out, hard as usual, sweating and smiling. After a brief exchange of pleasantries and some good-natured teasing, we went our separate ways on what seemed to be just another day, without any sense of what that day would bring.

Although I am filled with a range of emotions about the day I lost my friend, I am forever grateful that I got to spend so much one-on-one time with Daniel both in Hawaii and in Iraq. I learned a lot from his example, by the way he carried himself, and faced down challenges. I appreciate having been able to talk through challenges I faced, and for always being able to count on him and to lean on him.

While I may not remember the first time I met him, I will never forget Daniel Hyde. In honor of my friend, my wife Lesley and I wanted to name our first born son Owen Daniel. Owen means young warrior, and we are honored that our young warrior can carry on Daniel's legacy in name and some day in spirit.

OWEN DANIEL COLWELL was born on January 20, 2017, behind enemy lines in Annapolis, MD, to R. J. and Lesley Colwell.

BEAT NAVY!

GUY

On a sunny day many years ago at La Loma Jr. High School Daniel Hyde was shooting hoops during his fifth period lunch. I happened by and asked Daniel if I could shoot with him. The two of us started playing Horse and 21 until the bell called us back to class. This was the beginning of an incredibly quiet friendship.

Daniel and I continued to play basketball at lunch time in eighth grade and once Daniel's first year of freshmen football concluded at Thomas Downey High School, we found ourselves together again on the basketball court.

I realized early on that Daniel and I had something in common, an intense focus and drive for the game of basketball. As I continued to play, practice, go to open gym, and summer league basketball with Daniel, I realized Daniel was a polite, humble person. Daniel was not the best basketball player nor the most athletic, but I could see that Daniel's determination and work ethic were going to allow him to become a good athlete.

Having zero classes together at Downey High School because Daniel was way too smart for me to be able to keep up, our friendship and respect for one another was developing on the basketball court. While others joked around and goofed off at practice, Daniel and I were quiet and focused, probably even shy. I remember that Daniel, being the perfectionist he was, did not even like to mess up at practice. As others were more relaxed and had fun, Daniel and I tried to figure out how to be the best players we could be.

My sophomore year I was moved up to the Varsity team. That year my relationship and interaction with Daniel was different because we played on separate teams. Then we were joined again as teammates for our junior and senior years.

In Guy and Daniel's Senior year just as basketball season was getting underway, I remember Daniel telling me one day that Coach had announced that Guy would be missing a practice because he was at the hospital with his girlfriend having their baby. This emphasizes exactly how quiet and private Guy was. I am not sure any of his teammates knew they were expecting since Guy's girlfriend attended a different high school. Daniel told me that Coach asked them to vote if they wanted Guy to be allowed to start that week's game as usual since he had missed one practice. Guy started every game; however, Coach's rule was if you miss practice for any reason, you won't be starting the following game. When the team found out WHY Guy had missed practice and obviously so aware of Guy's talent on the court, they (I am sure) unanimously voted for Guy to start in the game as usual.

Daughter Riley was born to Guy and Sameth (Sam) on January 7 of 2003 and Daniel met baby Riley in February that year.

Guy's wife Sam recalls Daniel holding Riley for the first time at a home game in February. A bond was being formed with this baby and Daniel that would bring about a beautiful story in the years that followed.

Upon Daniel's first break back to California from West Point he made a point to look up Guy and Sam and check in on Riley. Daniel called Guy and met up with him before Guy's practice at Modesto Junior College. They shot around and played for an hour before Guy had to go to practice. A couple days later Guy had a game in Fairfield and Guy told Sam she should carpool with Daniel to come to the game. MapQuest (remember those days?) not being as reliable as it should have been, Daniel got lost and he and Sam arrived at the game just as Guy and the team were making their way to the bus to head home. Daniel didn't get to watch Guy play that night after all.

As Guy relayed his memories of his friendship with Daniel, he told me how he was so thankful for basketball. He realizes that without the game he may have never been introduced to Daniel and allowed to form a bond that has become stronger and has continued to grow even after Daniel's death.

Guy, being a true friend to Daniel and with unwavering support from his wife Sam, have educated their growing family about Daniel. All three children are being taught about Daniel's commitment to the military and ultimately his sacrifice. Guy and his family have made many trips to Lakewood Memorial Park to visit Daniel and show their gratitude.

Riley was six when Daniel was killed. As a little girl growing up, she heard many stories about Daniel. Sam said there was always a picture of Daniel in their home and as Riley would ask questions Guy and Sam would answer them.

Fast forward a few years to when Riley was trying out for basketball in eighth grade at Roosevelt Jr. High. She decided she wanted to try to obtain Daniel's high school basketball number (21) and wear it to respect, remember, represent, and honor Daniel, this friend of her parents, who lost his life in Iraq. Riley's dad Guy was a basketball legend at Thomas Downey High School as well as his years at Modesto Junior College: Point Guard, three-point shooter, quiet, always there, always making the shots. A LEGEND.

For Riley to get first choice on her jersey number she would have to make the most three-point shots. Riley wanted to wear Daniel's number in seventh grade but someone else beat her out for number 21. Persistence paid off because Riley practiced her shooting all summer and in eighth grade, she was able to choose the number 21. When Riley began her freshmen year at Thomas Downey High School, she was immediately moved up to play on the Varsity team. She played varsity her sophomore year as well. Both of those years she shot for number 21 and both years she got it.

Riley's junior year brought about a change with the ordering of new basketball uniforms. No number 21 had been ordered. Riley was handed the number 15. Unhappy but trying to work through her *emotions while doodling in class the following day Riley wrote out Daniel's full name, DANIEL BRIAN HYDE. For some reason she counted the letters and they added up to 15. At that moment Riley felt some peace regarding her new jersey number.*

Riley's senior year, 2020-2021, was the year our country was hit with the global pandemic, COVID-19. Sports were not being allowed in the fall of 2020 and students were homeschooling. Riley began training privately with her dad who was just starting up his own coaching / training business. In mid-March of 2021, the students went back to the classroom and all sports had a "mini season" with a few games scheduled. This is not the way any of us wanted Riley to end her high school basketball days but as the world can attest, we had no control.

Riley is special. Although her dad was a superstar in basketball and Daniel was an average player, Riley chose to honor Daniel in such a special and meaningful way.

Guy and Sam were expecting a baby boy in November of 2017. This baby boy would be their second son and third child. As if this wonderful family had not done enough, they decided to go for the dunk and give their baby boy our family's name.

Anakin (In Native American translates to Soldier) Hyde Ten Fingers was to be the baby's name.

Since the birth of this little "guy" and Riley playing basketball to honor Daniel, I made it a point to develop a better relationship with the family. It is remarkable and significant that two kids ages 17 & 18 had a baby together while in high school and have managed to stay together and have two more children. Guy and Sam are two of the most gracious, humble individuals I know. They work hard to provide for their family and are present parents whose children will remember that no matter what mom and dad were always THERE.

I am proud to know this family and proud of them. I realize and observe the way Guy and Sam treat one another with a kindness and gentleness that is unique. They have grown up together, are raising lovely children, and still speak and treat one another with grace and soft-spoken adoration.

ANAKIN HYDE TEN FINGERS was born on November 6, 2017, in Modesto, CA, to Guy and Sameth Ten Fingers.

TAILS OF VALOR
PAWS OF HONOR

FUR BABY HYDE

On February 5, 2018, a little black Labrador was born to bring good into the world. He was rescued by a program called Tails of Valor Paws of Honor, Inc. This organization, based in Pennsylvania, rescues dogs and trains them, and if they graduate from the program, they will be a service dog to veterans suffering from post-traumatic stress disorder (PTSD). Not only does the program rescue dogs and train them for service but they also name each dog in memory of a fallen hero.

Suzy Jones, the mother of Captain Jason Jones, a West Point classmate of Daniel's who lost his life in Afghanistan, along with Jason's high school friends, established a Foundation in memory of Jason (info@captainjasonjones.com). Jason's Foundation board members voted to sponsor a service dog for Jason AND for Daniel. Suzy contacted me, set the paws in motion, and stayed current on Hyde, the dog's name, throughout his training and graduation.

Jones and Hyde were rescued by the Tails of Valor program at the same time and were both puppies.

Hyde graduated for service on September 8, 2019, in Quakertown, PA. Hyde serves a Vietnam and Persian Gulf veteran, who retired after 24 Years of service in the Air Force. Hyde has improved the quality of life for his veteran to the best possible quality of life he can have as he is suffering from early-stage dementia. Hyde's veteran has a full-time caretaker and the two of them love Hyde and treat him like their child. Hyde lives in a beautiful home and his service is greatly appreciated.

What a special program that enhances not only the lives of the dogs they rescue but also of the veterans who have served our country. What an incredible honor to have Hyde serving in this way.

Puppy Hyde in the early stages of his training.

Service Dog Hyde on graduation day with Suzy Jones, the mother of
Jason Jones, whose Foundation sponsored Hyde's training

JENNY AND DEREK

Daniel met Jenny Labrum in the seventh grade at La Loma Junior High School. According to Jenny, Daniel made a first impression with her that she tries to re-play towards others every opportunity she gets. On her first day at La Loma, Daniel noticed Jenny standing alone and befriended her immediately. Jenny had gone to elementary school in Turlock, CA, where both of her parents were teachers. When Jenny began junior high in Modesto, she literally did not know a soul. We all know that trying to "fit in" to a new group is difficult. Imagine kids that have all gone to school together since they were five years old and not being willing to allow that "new girl" in. From that first day in seventh grade Daniel and Jenny became fast friends.

The following year in eighth grade Jenny was elected President of California Junior Scholarship Federation (CJSF) and Daniel was her sidekick Vice-President. For six years Daniel and Jenny sat together in college prep classes, and both remained active in leadership throughout their high school days. Jenny was a cheerleader while Daniel played football and basketball. Jenny and her fellow cheerleaders had a special little tradition they would do each time Daniel appeared at the free throw line. Before he shot Daniel would twist on the ball of his right foot from side to side as if putting out a cigarette butt, though he never smoked a day in his life! Daniel was the only player that had a whole team of cheerleaders mimicking his superstitious free throw routine. The girls knew Daniel would do this each time and began to anticipate it by doing the same gesture just before and as Daniel was shooting. Parted by college Jenny and Daniel stayed in touch through social media.

Derek also met Daniel in junior high at La Loma, but they became great friends playing high school football together. Four years of football games - forty games total. They had a total of four WINS in those four years. That adds up to a LOT of losses. The integrity of athletes that will continue to stand after falling so many times is impressive. It is easy to come back again and again to a winning team but to continue to show up when you consistently lose demonstrates a true warrior spirit. Derek and Daniel fought that battle together. They came back each year forming a bond for life. A friendship broken only because Daniel lost his life too soon.

On his short breaks from West Point, Daniel would always make time to stop by and catch up with Derek. Often that meant simply sitting in a room together watching sports and not uttering a single word to one another. They understood each other.

Derek showed up at our house the night we were notified about Daniel and became our rock and vital resource helping plan and carry out Daniels's wishes. He was at our home every single day following the most horrific night of our lives and throughout both services two weeks later. Derek delivered a memorable speech at Daniel's Celebration of Life Service. After that he stopped in to check on us regularly.

Derek and Jenny were brought together again after years separated when they both attended Daniel's services. Following one of them, the young people all met up at a bar downtown. Derek and Jenny spent quite a while that night catching up.

Jenny was living in Newport Beach at the time and attending Physician Assistant school through a program at Pomona. That being her second year, she was not required to live in Pomona since she was doing clinical rotations in various hospitals.

When Daniel's services concluded, Jenny returned to Newport and was greeted by a message from Derek. He expressed his enjoyment spending time with her again and catching up after so many years. Derek told Jenny if he had learned one thing so far from Daniel's death it was that nothing is ever guaranteed, and you should tell people how you feel about them. Derek told Jenny that night he had always hoped they would end up together someday.

As a result, Derek and Jenny continued to stay in touch and after Jenny graduated from the P.A. program in July of 2009, she left Newport and moved to Connecticut to begin her P.A. residency at Yale University. Derek eventually got on a plane to visit Jenny in Connecticut for their "first official date." For their second date they met up in Mexico which was about an equal traveling distance for both.

When Jenny completed her residency, she accepted a job at New York Presbyterian where she was working in cardiac surgery. Jenny held that position for two years and kept extremely busy. Derek continued to visit when he could.

Jenny eventually took a position in Walnut Creek, California, where she and Derek were able to pursue their relationship on a more serious level without an air commute. As time went by Derek and Jenny got an apartment in Walnut Creek and as it has been said…the rest is history.

Derek and Jenny married in June of 2017.

At the conclusion of the fabulous festivities on Derek's and Jenny's wedding day, Derek sat down with Brian and me to assure us that it had been Daniel that brought he and Jenny together.

On March 7, 2018, an incredibly special baby girl made her way into the world.

Derek and Jenny, nine years *to the day* after Daniel's death in Iraq, welcomed their baby girl Emerson into the world. I truly cannot think of a more radiant light looking over Jenny, Derek, and Emerson - from Daniel.

I know with my entire soul that Daniel is so proud and elated that these two wonderful friends found their way to one another and became a family of five, with two children, Emerson and Everett, and their doodle, Nana.

SURPRISE!

In December of 2018 I received a Facebook message from one of Daniel's junior high school friends. Megan and Daniel had met at sixth grade camp since Sonoma and Lakewood schools attended camp at the same time. They reconnected when they both attended La Loma Jr. High School. They used to eat lunch together in Mr. Constable's classroom and Megan remembers Daniel eating healthy lunches and talking about his martial arts pursuit to higher belt levels.

Megan, at the time of her message to me, was employed at Modesto Junior College and had recently finished reading my first book. It took her six years after its publication to pick it up and read it. Without knowing why it took her that long, she messaged me to tell me her reaction to the book after starting and finishing it in one sitting.

A couple months later Megan mentioned my book to her boss who also purchased a copy and read it. Megan and Bryan served the Campus Life, Student Learning, and Veterans Services Offices of the College. Bryan asked Megan if she thought I might be interested in coming to Modesto to speak about Daniel and about our experiences since his death.

Being the 10-year anniversary of Daniel's death, the timing could not have been better. It made sense for me to be in Modesto in March to visit Daniel's grave. I try to take every opportunity to speak about Daniel when I am asked to do so.

The Junior College had been hosting a series of evenings with local authors. Megan and Bryan thought my story would be a great fit. When Megan told me the date of the event it solidified it for me. I would be speaking on March 13th, 2019. Those 13s always make their way to us.

I got busy writing my speech. I have spoken several times about Daniel at different events. I always write a new speech. The events normally have a different type of focus and there are always new things to tell so I write accordingly. I learned how to write speeches from Coach Bill McHale, Daniel's basketball coach.

The first time I was asked to speak about Daniel was Memorial Weekend 14 months after his death. I knew I would need help organizing and practicing. I sought out the help of Daniel's coach, who taught English, and had spoken beautifully at Daniel's service. Although he became emotional while he was speaking, his speech was eloquent, meaningful, heartfelt, and organized. I knew he was the person to ask for help. I wrote a rough draft and Bill edited it. Then I rewrote and Bill edited. We did this so many times I lost count. Finally, Bill said, "At some point we need to say this is done." He assured me he could edit until the end of time, but I needed to rehearse the speech and commit to not changing it. Bill directed me to read it over a few times and then to come to school to practice it aloud. I did not want to do this. I was mortified. He said the only way to get past the parts that might make me emotional was to say it ALOUD repeatedly. Then he probably made some joke about how unfortunately that did not work out for him on the day of Daniel's service. Bill said he would have a student or two in the classroom so I could give the speech to kids that did not know anything about Daniel. Nervously I did what he asked, and it was not so bad. Once I got going, I was surprisingly comfortable and confident.

I learned over time that I loved speaking. I was good at it. I do not become emotional, and I am SO PROUD to have the honor of telling listeners about my son.

Bill is a fabulous teacher and I learned to be a good speaker because he taught me how to be good at it. Bill taught me to write out the speech word for word, practice it so many times that looking down is infrequent, and to print it in LARGE type so it would always be easy to find my place.

I wanted my upcoming speech to be special so I contemplated long and hard about the direction I would take. Soon I received another message that gloriously gave me the answer I needed.

THORPE

Facebook Messenger

January 1, 2019 5:18 pm

Mrs. Hyde

My name is Thorpe Facer and I served with your son during his time in Iraq. Over the past two days I have read the book you have written about his incredible life. It's a beautiful and well-written book. I've put this off for so long. I'm not sure why, maybe I'm hiding from it or running from it, maybe it's because compared to others in my unit I had very little interaction with your son and felt that their grief took priority over mine.

I knew LT Hyde fleetingly. I met him twice, but only once when he was aware of it. I was heading home for leave hoping to make it home in time to see my first child born.

The night before, I was shaving in the shared restroom when your son came in. He was new to the unit, and I didn't know who he was. He was in PT uniform (work-out wear) with no rank. We greeted each other and we started talking. I can't remember about what just trivial things. However, one thing I do remember was laughing a lot and thinking this new guy was going to fit right in.

Only after I had wrapped up in the restroom did he mention his name and rank. I knew then that leadership ran in his blood. For many officers, this kind of interaction would have remained formal, but not for him. I felt like I was talking to a friend. I didn't realize then how much I would replay that conversation in my head in the weeks to come.

I went on leave and upon arrival back in Iraq, I was immediately told to gear up, we had wounded, and we were to escort them back to the patrol base. I don't remember much after that; it was a blur and things happened quickly.

When the news of his death came out, we were devastated. It was painful. I barely knew your son, but he was a brother in arms and that's a bond that transcends blood.

I can't imagine your pain, I can't relate to your pain, but most of all I wish that you never had to endure this pain.

Your book helped me in a way I can't explain. Over my military career, I lost many friends to combat, but your son's loss bothers me the most. It bothers me because I will always wonder what could have been. What I could have learned from him and how he could have helped me to grow. It's something I will never know. Well, I thought I would never know. Then I read your book and realized that even in the short time I knew him he taught me many things. He taught me that sacrifice, while painful, is noble. He taught me to be a better person and to live life to the fullest without saying a single word. He reminds me every day to make life mean something in honor of him and those other friends I lost.

My second son, born roughly two years after Daniel's death, is named Jayce Daniel Facer. His middle name is in remembrance of your son.

Thank you. Thank you for raising an incredible son and thank you for writing the book about his life. Thank you for helping me to heal.

Sincerely,
Thorpe A. Facer II

JAYCE DANIEL FACER was born on January 19, 2011, in Urbana, IL, to Brittanney Merath and Thorpe Facer II and currently resides with Thorpe and Cassie Facer.

I could hardly believe my teary eyes. Another namesake? I had just received the best surprise ending for my speech at the college, a baby born two years after Daniel died, named after him, and unknown to us for eight years.

On that unforgettable evening of March 13, in room 113, I delivered my speech. My husband said it was the best delivery he had heard in the 10 years I had been speaking about Daniel. It was incredibly exciting to share Daniel's namesakes and the unbelievable joy that he had been honored by the parents of eight boys in 10 years.

At the end of my speech, we had planned for a question-and-answer session. As we conversed about many things, I could not keep myself from repeating, "Can you believe it? Eight boys in 10 years!"

Ali slowly stood up with her young son and in a shaky, quiet voice said, "Glenda...you have 9!"

★

THE DAY I MET ALI

I met Ali six days *before* my speech at the college, on March 7, 2019. Since I was in Modesto for the speech, I had mentioned on social media that I was planning to visit Daniel's grave in the afternoon of the seventh. I love to see my fantastic village of friends from Modesto, so I posted a specific time to gather. Several people came even in the rain, and it was uplifting to see everyone.

Ali's husband had been attending Stanford University to obtain his master's degree. Ali first visited Daniel's grave their first Memorial Day in California, May of 2018. She had contacted me via Facebook to tell me she had done so. She elaborated that she and her twin boys had a lovely day at the Memorial Park. Ali spent time that day telling the boys about her dear friend, Daniel, who had been killed in Iraq. The twins were three years old at the time.

Ali, who attended West Point and was one year older than Daniel, and I had arranged to meet at Daniel's grave in the morning before the other Modesto friends were scheduled to arrive. While we talked Ali did her best to keep the boys occupied with a video so she could finally tell me a little about her relationship with Daniel. She had mentioned the boys' names: Ezra and Daniel. I did not give their names much thought as I cannot just assume that every child given the name Daniel by a parent who knew my Daniel, has anything to do with my Daniel…or should I?

Ali and I talked for a long while on that cold, damp, day in March and Ali became emotional several times trying to express her feelings about Daniel and their time together both at West Point and in Iraq.

R.J. Colewell had also made a special trip to visit Daniel's grave that day with his wife, Lesley and their son, Owen Daniel. R.J. was a roommate, fellow officer, and great friend of Daniel's, and their son, Owen Daniel, is a namesake. R.J. had been to Daniel's grave before but this was the first time for his wife and son. Ali and R.J. were friends, fellow officers in the Army, and both in Iraq when Daniel was killed. The two of them had discussed meeting at the same time at Daniel's gravesite and then taking me to have lunch with them.

I remember being surprised at how active Ali's twins were. At one point I said something as I laughed like, "I can't believe his name is Daniel. He is so much busier than my Daniel ever was." I TRULY HAD NO IDEA. Well, if poor Ali had planned to try and tell me that day that her Daniel *was* named after *my* Daniel, I had pretty much just taken that opportunity away. Later, at lunch with Ali, R.J., Lesley, and the three boys, I apologized to Ali. I said, "I didn't mean to sound degrading about the twins' busy behavior." Ali was so understanding even commenting that the boys were active little guys. She knew my Daniel quite well and understood my comment because of his calm demeanor. My son, Daniel, was calm from the beginning. When our daughter was born and had a strong opinion about things, I was taken aback even though Andrea was also quite easy. SHE seemed so different to me than her brother was. My Daniel was unusual in his calmness even as a child.

Although Ali's twins were already three, Ali had not been able to speak to me about the twins or my Daniel because it was still raw and extremely difficult for her 10 years later.

As we were saying goodbye after lunch, Ali said she was planning to come and hear me speak at the junior college and she would be bringing her oldest, Daniel, with her. Ali showed up at the JC on the evening of my speech, however, I did not get a chance to chat with her before the event started. Young Daniel sat perfectly quiet the entire time I was speaking.

I still had no clue that Ali would gather the courage to SURPRISE me that evening, surprise all of us, with her unexpected, wonderful news.

ALI

I met Dan at West Point when we served together on Brigade staff and lived on the same floor of Eisenhower barracks. At the time, he was serving as Brigade staff's First Sergeant, which was a challenging job for him. He was assigned to make sure the Brigade staff - the highest-ranking cadets in the corps who were all seniors - were accounted for, wearing their uniforms properly, and upholding standards in general.

Dan was good at the job because he had the perfect blend of humility and social/leadership skills: He could get people to listen to him without pissing them off. He always had a big smile for everyone as he went around inspecting their rooms, asking people how they were, genuinely caring more about their responses than what their rooms looked like.

My roommate and I began calling Dan "the Most Eligible Bachelor" because he was THE nicest guy and we knew he would make some lady very happy one day. Each time he came to our room to inspect it, we would tease him and tell him this, and Dan would just grin with his big, shy smile, and shake his head.

That school year, Dan was chosen to participate in a summer key leader board in which the Brigade Tactical Officer, all the regimental tactical officers, First Captain Stephanie Hightower, and the Brigade Command Sergeant Major (myself) interviewed the top cadets in the class of 2007 to determine who would hold the top leadership positions in the next summer's training. After hearing from 40-50 cadets, and having the difficult task of ranking them, Stephanie and I both - individually, without collaboration beforehand - put Dan at the very top of our lists. Dan ended up ranking in the top four and was therefore assigned a Regimental Commander position for the summer.

Dan remained on Brigade staff for his entire junior year at West Point, later serving as a Color Sergeant - specifically, the one who had the honor to carry the American flag during cadet parades. I remember Dan was extremely diligent with academics. We'd often find him studying in the Brigade staff conference room, as the seniors who surrounded him did everything except quietly study, especially as their year was ending. Dan never seemed upset or irritated at how loud it was and was so patient with all our nonsense.

Two years after I graduated, I reconnected with Dan as he was arriving in Hawaii. He was assigned to the same brigade that I was and moved in with my good friend and "mom" away from home, Danny Hwang. The three of us spent a lot of time together in the weeks leading up to our deployment to Iraq. We attended church, shared family dinners, and spent weekends together dancing, going to clubs, and attending parties. We made plans to live on the North Shore after we returned from the deployment.

Dan remained a good friend to me during a very difficult time in my life in the months preceding our deployment to Iraq. He was patient, kind, and never judgmental. He always listened through my sometimes-tearful rantings, ensured I always had a dance partner or someone to talk to while we were out, made certain I got home safely on more than one occasion, and remained a faithful friend no matter what.

The night before I left for Iraq, I saw Dan, hugged him, and told him goodbye and to take care of himself. Dan immediately replied, "You be safe," even though we both knew I would be in a safer place than Dan would be. I saw Dan once more in Kuwait before our final push into Iraq, and we had breakfast together in the chow hall.

I've replayed the last few weeks in Hawaii and that last breakfast in Kuwait over and over in my head a million times. I wish I would have told Dan more, seen him more often, or communicated with him more regularly via Facebook once we deployed. As we all do, I thought I would have more time.

I learned of Dan's death while I was sitting at my desk in Iraq working as an intelligence officer for an adjacent battalion. An e-mail message came through detailing a horrific attack that had just occurred in his area of operations. My heart sank and my stomach dropped as I somehow felt immediately certain he was one of the U.S. soldiers involved. I ran next door to ask our battle captain to try to get the names of the injured. Later that evening, a senior officer pulled me out of my office and confirmed the worst news I'd ever received.

In the years following Dan's death, I was filled with regret and shame for what had been left unsaid and how I felt I had wasted so much time because I was stuck in my own mess. I tried everything I could to live my life to the fullest, in a way that would make Dan proud and honor his life. I ran marathons and triathlons. I climbed Mt. Kilimanjaro. I volunteered to deploy as part of the Cultural Support Team program and supported direct action units (Rangers and Special Operations) to get as close as I could to affecting the fight against the terrorist ideology that took Dan's life.

After several years, I realized my friendship with Dan changed my life. I wore Dan's KIA bracelet every day, on every mission, in every race, in every workout for motivation, as a constant reminder to *never accept mediocrity in any aspect of my life*, and to remember that every day is a gift, and to treat everyone I loved as if it were my last day and the last time I would see them. Dan had inspired me to live a more fulfilling life and his faith led me to recommit my life to Christ after years of spiritual stagnation. I eventually met a man who loved the Lord, respected me, and who, as Dan always would, just listened to me.

Prior to a deployment to Afghanistan, I wrote a letter to Jonathan, my newfound love (and future husband), explaining how Dan played a huge part in my volunteering for this job and what Dan had meant to me as a friend and someone I cared deeply for. I wanted him to know exactly who Dan was and how he had influenced my life in so many positive ways. I had learned, through Dan's untimely death, that we must appreciate the people we love and tell them so, often, because one never knows when they may lose the opportunity to express their most honest feelings, when suddenly, it is too late. I wanted to put it all down in writing this time, just in case.

In 2015, I was pregnant with twins, and Jonathan and I struggled to agree on names. I never suggested the name "Daniel" to Jonathan because I wasn't sure if my husband could understand why I would want to name my son after another man. Then, two weeks before the boys were born, my husband being the incredible and intuitive man that he is, recalled the letter I wrote him and suggested the name Daniel…for me. Immediately we had one baby named Daniel and the other to be named Ezra.

I wanted to be sure the "correct" twin got the name Daniel. We agreed to wait until we met both boys to decide who was who. However, while I carried the boys, I always felt one of them had a stronger "Daniel" personality. He was the twin (baby A) who was more active of the two, the one who moved constantly day and night, and the one who probably broke one of my ribs with his leg presses! My firstborn, by two minutes, was THE Daniel for sure.

I am thankful that my son Daniel has the role model of Daniel Hyde. I am excited for him to read about Daniel and learn about the kind of person he was named for. I often talk to young Daniel about Dan and the values he stood for. I pray his name will keep him strong, principled, inspired, and grounded for his entire life.

DANIEL EDWARD KRALICK was born on August 13, 2015, in Raleigh, NC, to Ali and Jonathan Kralick.

JONATHAN

Not only did Ali's husband, Jonathan, give Ali the "go" on naming their firstborn Daniel, but Jonathan was also the founder in 2019 of the Daniel Hyde Memorial Symposium at West Point.

As an Instructor and Course Director for MC306 Dynamics, a Mechanical Engineering course, Jonathan was responsible for implementing the Symposium.

This biannual Symposium highlights design projects where engineering students model a real-world problem with dynamics analysis and differential equations at the end of their semester-long course. Engineers must be able to translate challenging real-world problems into manageable components for qualitative analysis. The problem solving also translates directly into the cadets upcoming role as commissioned officers in the US ARMY which requires that they are able to understand, analyze, and solve complex problems. Jonathan's intention was to ensure that the cadets in the class understood the importance of learning the material to earn their degree but also appreciate the greater context for why they needed to solve problems as leaders in the Army.

In Jonathan's own words, "Daniel Hyde embodied this problem-solving mentality. As a civil engineer he was not required to take this Dynamics course but chose to because of his love of learning and desire to be better. He excelled in this challenging course, ultimately earning an A - an above average grade. During his time in the Army, he continued to lead through challenging problems, demonstrating his commitment to excellence, and not accepting mediocrity in any aspect of his life. Memorializing Daniel's legacy through this Symposium has provided the cadets an opportunity to culminate their dynamics course and appreciate their upcoming role as an Army officer. Cadets learn about Daniel when they receive the assignment half-way through the course and learn more about his service and sacrifice at the Symposium".

An excerpt from the student assignment handout:

Daniel Hyde graduated from the USMA in 2007 with a degree in Civil Engineering. His A in ME306 (Dynamics precursor to MC306) demonstrates his engineering acumen and love for learning especially since it was a voluntary elective during the 2nd semester of his firstie year. Daniel applied his problem-solving skill set, attention to detail, and desire to serve as an infantry platoon leader in 25th Infantry Division. Friends remember his cheerful personality, willingness to lend you a hand, and his tenacious desire to excel at any task regardless of the difficulty. Daniel was killed in action 7 March 2009 in Tikrit, Iraq.

> *Our family is extremely grateful to Jonathan for this gift: memorializing Daniel's tenacity for learning, desire to excel in everything, and his demonstration of ability to think outside his own engineering box.*

VETERANS MEMORIAL MUSEUM

In August of 2019, my dad's side of my family met in Branson, MO, for our traditional family reunion. We try to gather every three years at a different location to enjoy the family that remains and remember those that have gone.

My Aunt Geri and Uncle Roger had contacted Veterans Memorial Museum in Branson to see if they would be interested in receiving memorabilia of Daniel's for display. The museum was extremely interested, and I decided to send them Daniel's green uniform since it had been discontinued. The museum wanted a "theme" or legacy story for the display, and I could not think of anything more substantial than the (at that time) nine boys that had been given Daniel's name.

I loved the idea that Daniel's uniform would be forever preserved and appreciated. I contacted the museum, received my instructions, and the generous staff committed to having the display ready when our family arrived so we could tour the museum with the display for Daniel completed.

My Uncle Wayne, Daniel's great Uncle, had served in the US ARMY and his uniform was also displayed at this museum. We thought it so touching that Daniel's uniform would remain there with my dad's brother's uniform. Check out the patch on the shoulder of Uncle Wayne's uniform. No one in the family remembered or knew of the patch, and believe me, when we saw it, we were spellbound.

Wayne W. Meyer served in New Guinea and the Philippines.

Daniel's uniform display in Branson, Missouri.

BRANDON

The name Caleb Daniel Thomas has a nice ring to it. Why is it relevant you ask? Well, because Caleb was the first scout in the bible, and he dared to tell the truth. Also, because Daniel Brian Hyde was my roommate while I was at West Point. If you do not know Dan, please take a moment to check out Glenda Hyde's book, *24 Years and 40 Days: The Story of Army 1LT Daniel Hyde.* Dan and I were classmates in the Class of 2007. We happened to come from the same Regiment and both of us were recommended to represent the United States Military Academy as members of the Color Guard.

During our first meeting, we got sized up and I ended up with the honor of being shoulder-to-shoulder with Dan. Dan bore the National Flag and I was his Rifle Guard. We had two vastly different positions training-wise, but from the moment I met the dude from Cali, I knew he was different. Dan had this quiet way about him, some might call it a stern demeanor, but he was focused and jovial at heart. Dan was the type of guy that just went with the flow, so long as the flow was the right way. I was going through an interesting period in my life, my parents were separating and introspectively I was seeking the light. Throughout my challenges that year, Dan was solid as a rock. Roommates at West Point are a weird thing. In the grand scheme of things, I dearly love all of them and cherish the memories we made as "forced friends" for four to six months at a time! However, I can say that in the moment it can be a crapshoot, especially coming to a new unit like Brigade Staff, but I always lucked out.

Dan and I were never best friends, but you get to know a guy and become friends when you drill day in and day out to be sharp. Sometimes our team of five would practice long after the rest of the Corps finished drill. Mostly it was because Dan would kind of drop a hint in his, "Well, I think we can do it a little better" way. He was never demanding, but the little nudge was just enough that we all wanted to try that much harder to get things right.

Before we all signed our names to the barracks color room, a time-honored tradition, we ended up all agreeing with Dan that we should have lines stenciled on the wall first to keep things level and organized, but that was Dan for you. He just had this presence.

So why name my kid after Dan? Well, because he is, and forever will be, a hero. He stood in the gap that gives me and every one of you in America reading this, the freedoms you enjoy. We live the saying "Freedom isn't free" because Dan paid the ultimate price, like many of my other classmates and friends. I did it to honor him, his memory, and hopefully to have his story and legacy live on. I also pray that my son has a little bit of Dan's attention as his guardian angel. There are many more stories to share about Dan, but the bottom line is that he was somebody that I and many others looked up to, and who did not hesitate to be there for you. I feel like in this small way, I can be there for him.

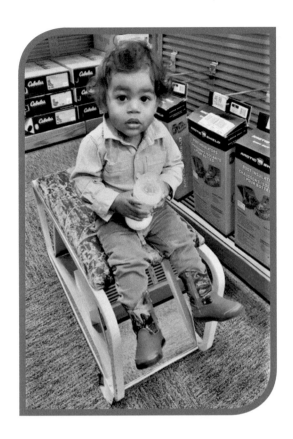

A story for my son, Caleb Daniel...

One time we were standing waiting to execute a parade as the color guard. We always had an area in a sally port near the central guard room. The Central Guardroom (CGR) is where we cadets had to pull guard duty and answer phones as the "HQ" for all the cadets, and sometimes packages would arrive there. That is all anyone really cared about from CGR. So, we normally stood around in a loose line, but not Dan. From the time we left our room in full dress for missions, Dan was game-on. Our West Point insert photographer was floating around and snapped several shots of Dan's reflection and the reflection of the flag from Dan's brass buckle after we uncased the colors. Dan was like a statue the whole time and as I recall, I was reminded of a toy tin soldier in grey and white. The buckle was meticulous. The night before, Dan and I stayed up after his problem sets just shinning all our brass. Dan showed me this trick where he heated the Brasso off a new buckle to get the varnish off and down to the metal faster and I thought I was MacGyver. Anyway, his brass was danged shiny, and I was proud, yet again to stand in his shadow (quite literally).

CALEB DANIEL THOMAS was born on October 7, 2019, in Plano, TX, to Brandon and Christina Thomas.

MATT

As a team of Daniel's peers and our family began working to build the Daniel Hyde Memorial Foundation in early 2020, I posted an announcement of its early developmental stages on Daniel's Facebook page.

A young man by the name of Matt Briggs commented on the post. He said it was exciting news about the foundation and that Dan had been a Firstie (senior) during his Plebe (freshmen) year. Matt went on to say that Dan had a profound impact on him through a small handful of acts of kindness and mentorship. He continued his comments saying he never had a chance to thank Dan, but that his son's middle name was Daniel. Matt said he is excited to teach his son about Dan's example as his son gets older.

I had to find out more. I tried to be as subtle and unassuming as possible.

I sent Matt a private message to ask if his son's middle name was a result of my Daniel's influence. Matt's answer was, "The two biggest influences in my military career were both named Daniel, your son being one of them. So yes, that is intentional."

I wanted to continue talking but Matt was up against a deadline for work. He said he would call me the following day if I was interested in providing my phone number. I could not send my phone number fast enough and the next day we chatted.

I told Matt about the book I was working on and asked if I could include his story and his son as one of Daniel's namesakes. He said they would be honored. I asked him to tell me about his relationship with Daniel. He did remember a couple of stories to tell me but gosh it had been 11 years and naturally his memories had faded.

As Matt and I continued talking he mentioned a tattoo he had on his midsection. Matt said that was the first thing he did on his spring break from the academy right after Dan died. I wanted to see the tattoo, but I gave him an out. I said if sending me a picture was too personal or uncomfortable no problem. Before I could finish typing I had a photograph.

As soon as I laid eyes on Matt's tattoo, I realized I had literally stumbled right onto my son's eleventh namesake. No doubt in my mind whatsoever this was not an accident.

Matt's tattoo (the best of us Dan Hyde)

I asked Matt to tell me a little bit about his remembrances of Daniel. Matt said Dan was a "big" important Regimental Commander and he was a lowly Plebe which is why he was so surprised by Dan's kindness and mentorship.

Matt was enlisted in the Army and had finished a deployment before he was discovered as a candidate for West Point. The "other" Daniel in his life was his battle buddy a couple years older than Matt who convinced Matt that if he would put forth some effort, he could become someone special. This Daniel pushed Matt to complete his application to West Point.

When Matt mentioned the times he encountered my Daniel, he said it was probably less than a few, but they were quite memorable. Once during intramural sports Matt was feeling discouraged. As a Plebe, but older because of late application to the academy, it was difficult to hear from his superiors what he needed to do when they were younger and inexperienced in the field, unlike Matt. He was telling Daniel that he was "about done" and my son encouraged him to trust the system. Daniel told Matt that "we" here at West Point have been around for a long time and "we" know what we are doing. He asked Matt to just apply himself and told him he would be okay. And he was.

Matt said there were just a couple of other times where he would run into Dan, and he always had a kind way about him, and he was always encouraging.

Matt knew that Dan was destined for leadership because he could lead by example without being a jerk. The other thing that really resonated with Matt was the day the academy heard the news of Dan Hyde's death In Iraq. He said in all his four years at the academy never can he remember such a somber, quiet, sad day as that one was. It became clear to him what an impact Dan Hyde had on so many others like himself.

KENNETH DANIEL BRIGGS was born on September 24, 2018, in Austin, TX to Matt and Rose Briggs.

KYLE

I first met Daniel when we both trained in karate at West Coast tae kwon do. I was five or six years old when I started there and, if I recall, Daniel was around the same age. We participated in many of the same karate training classes together, tested for various belts together, and we both eventually achieved the rank of black belt.

Throughout our adolescent years we followed along the same path. We went to the same junior high and high school, but Daniel was a year older than me, so we didn't have the same classes. However, we participated in many of the same extracurricular activities. In high school, we were both in leadership. Daniel was voted Student Body President by his peers for his junior and senior years. This was the first time someone had served as Student Body President over multiple school years at Downey High School, which is testament to Daniel's leadership qualities and how much people looked up to him. We played on the golf team together, and we both played basketball, though he was a much more gifted athlete.

People often asked me if we were brothers since we looked somewhat alike and did a lot of the same activities. I always looked up to Daniel - he just had that 'thing' about him. Anyone that knew him knows what I am talking about. He always stuck up for others and was a natural leader. In fact, I remember Daniel used to say that one day he planned to run for the office of the President of the United States. Now when friends talk, sometimes it is just that, talk. But when we would have these conversations, Daniel was matter-of-fact about it and I knew full and well that Daniel would be an incredible President. Each step he took during his adolescence was gearing him towards his goal to run for President.

Daniel never put anyone down or had a negative comment to say. In high school, it made me jealous to hear all the girls swooning over him! He was a gifted athlete, incredible student, and good looking. I mean, what wasn't there to like? There is no other way to put it other than, he was the cool kid that everyone wanted to be, including me.

Amongst everything else, the one thing that sticks out to me the most about Daniel is how he would go out of his way to say hi to someone and ask how their day was going. That is something you don't see a lot of folks doing these days, unfortunately, but it goes to show the kindness and maturity Daniel possessed.

Because Daniel was Daniel, he received a full scholarship for all three military academies (wow!). As we all know, he chose West Point. I graduated from Downey and pursued a business degree from CSU Fresno. After high school, I kept up with Daniel's endeavors through family and friends. It is cliché, but also true, that life gets in the way, and we, unfortunately, lose touch with good friends, as was the case with Daniel and me. It was nothing intentional, but I know the rigors of West Point kept Daniel busy and though I cannot say I was a straight A student at Fresno, I still kept busy with schoolwork, study abroad programs, and jobs.

Before Daniel's passing and well before ever becoming a father myself, Daniel was the one person I wanted and hoped my future kids would emulate. All parents want the world for their children and wish for them to become successful in life, but I thought that if I could raise my future kids to be only half of the person Daniel had become, that would be quite the accomplishment. I can only imagine how proud Glenda and Brian must be of the person that Daniel became.

I am now married to the love of my life and the father of two young children. Unless you are planning to name your child to be a Jr. or the III, every parent can attest that naming a child is no easy task! Some parents name their children after family members, such as a parent or grandparent. Some name them after famous athletes or movie stars. Some even pick names out of a hat. But there was never a doubt in my mind when it came to choosing our son's name. After sharing Daniel's story with my wife and explaining how much of an influence he had on me, and still does to this day, we were honored and humbled to name our son after him.

I certainly miss and think about Daniel Hyde often and I cannot wait until my kids are old enough for me to tell them about the incredible person, I had the privilege of knowing.

DANIEL ROY SHEPARDSON was born on March 6, 2020, in Modesto, CA, to Kyle and Cortney Shepardson.

THE DANIEL HYDE
MEMORIAL FOUNDATION

In March of 2019, in observance of the 10-year anniversary of Daniel's death, a group of his friends from West Point joined together to compete in a race outside of Las Vegas. Later that day several came to our home for an afternoon of food and fellowship.

We talked, laughed, ate, drank, and bonded once again as the larger family we have acquired since Daniel died. Although we miss Daniel every single day, our pain has been greatly diminished with the incredible people that have come into our lives.

Dan Lennox-Choate, a classmate and friend of Daniel's, competed in the half marathon event. Prior to the run, Dan decided to reach out on social media and share his plans to run in memory of Daniel. He collected roughly $5,000.00 in donations and realized then that something needed to be done to permanently honor Daniel's sacrifice.

Dan returned home and reached out to a couple other classmates. Together the three of them jumped through all the hoops to establish a Non-Profit, 501 (c) (3).

When the hard work was done, Dan gave our family a call and shared the great surprise that the FOUNDATION had been established. He suggested our family should come up with a name and that the six of us, the board, consider a project that would be worthy of Daniel's commitment to leadership and character.

The board met and ideas were tossed around. The board members constructed a plan and sought out the help of the West Point Association of Graduates, decided on a project, and began our fund-raising campaign.

With hard work, motivation, and during a global pandemic to boot, in just over one month we had raised the 100k needed to permanently endow an internship with the National Security Council. As a result, each year until the end of time one Cadet at West Point will be selected to receive this grand opportunity, thanks to the formation and execution of the DANIEL HYDE MEMORIAL FOUNDATION.

The Foundation Board members are Brian, Glenda, and Andrea Hyde, Daniel Lennox-Choate, Matthew Hoff, and JB Kelly. To these three men, Dan, Matt, and JB, who are all West Point classmates of Daniel, we owe a debt of gratitude for their service to our country, their hard work, their incredible brains, and their desire to honor our son/brother, their friend, in such a monumental way.

The Daniel Hyde Memorial Foundation
Hydememorialfoundation.org

Being part (a tiny part) of the development of the Hyde Memorial Foundation has given our family immense comfort. People, no matter how much love and attention they may receive after their death, will eventually, over great time, begin to fade. Being assured that Daniel will be remembered for his service and sacrifice every year until the absolute end of time means everything!

Having been blessed so incredibly with Daniel's namesakes, along about the tenth little guy, I began to wonder if there would ever be 13. I mean, how could that not run through my mind when 13 has been so prominent in our lives? It was such an important number to Daniel. I couldn't help but think how amazing it would be but also felt awful even having the thought, when each of these precious boys means so much to us. I didn't need more, expect more, anticipate more…I simply wondered.

On Friday, December 17, 2021, I received a very special text. It was a group text to all 5 Hyde Foundation Board members from the 6th board member, JB Kelly.

It contained a picture of a beautiful brand-new baby boy and the text read:

Elliott Daniel Kelly, 7 lbs. 7 oz.

Andrea was the first to respond, "He's beautiful, congrats to you both!!!"

JB

I met Dan our Plebe (freshmen) year. We were in the same company for the summer cadet basic training (BEAST) and the school year. I wouldn't say we were great friends that first summer, but second semester of the academic year we hung out a bit more. My fondest memories of Dan were messing with him on the weekends. He'd be doing homework on a Friday or Saturday night, and I would come in and goof around or mess something up in his room. His perfectly made bed was my most frequent target. It was always lighthearted, never mean, and I got the sense that Dan appreciated the break every now and then. After that first year, we all transferred companies and we were also different academic majors, so we drifted apart a bit but remained friendly. We touched base every now and again. We had some deeper conversations our junior year when I sought his advice while going through a significant roommate conflict. My roommate broke the cadet honor code doing something trivial, and I was looked down upon by some of my peers for speaking up about it.

Our senior year Dan and I reconnected while we were both on the cadet 4th regimental staff. Dan was the regimental commander, and Ben Flores and I were roommates on Daniel's staff, and lived down the hall from Dan. Ben and I both tried to push Dan to have a bit more fun and to remember to relax. One of my favorite memories was convincing Dan to come out with Ben and me to a football game tailgate party. When we arrived, we realized the event was hosted by the Lacrosse team and there was drinking, including underclassmen. Dan specifically got "intercepted" by one of the Lacrosse guys, who was concerned about Dan narcing on the underage drinking. The whole walk back, Dan was like, "Dude, I played high school football. They know I'm not that lame, right?"

Also, during routine formations that occurred almost daily, I as the cadet S1 was required to report (salute) to Dan since Dan was the Commander. There were formal things I was supposed to say to him, but I would always say the most ridiculous things to try to get him to laugh. He was great about holding his composure, however I managed to "get him" a few times.

Since we both branched Infantry, we did the same Officer training after West Point. We crossed paths in Ranger school when Dan was recycled back into my class in Florida. A few weeks before he was killed in action, we exchanged happy belated birthday wishes to one another as we both have winter birthdays.

I would never call myself one of Dan's best friends, but I do wonder how things would have turned out if he hadn't been killed. I'd like to think we'd still be good friends and I'd still be the goofball "messing" with the overachiever for some comic relief.

I appreciate how close I have become with Brian, Glenda, and Andrea. Dan's passing taught me a lot, maybe the most, about the social aspects of dealing with death in general. I very much doubt I would know Glenda, Brian, and Andrea to the level I do now, and I cherish those relationships. I always knew OF the Hydes but in a secondary, indirect way. I think if there is a lesson or takeaway here, I learned to be open to letting those secondary connections become primary, direct connections because there's so much value and healing in that.

I couldn't be more honored to be part of establishing the Hyde Memorial Foundation and will continue my role of saying sarcastic things that piss off someone named Daniel on a semi-regular basis.

I met my wife, Mandy, in Germany. I was strung out after three years of being deployed every six months and, during the six months at home, we would train our asses off. At the time German culture wasn't exactly friendly to American soldiers. Mandy and I met when I had a more stable staff job my last year in Germany. Mandy had moved from Korea to work in a hospital in Germany. We spent every weekend together our first year and, when I moved back to the U.S., Mandy stayed in Germany. It was the kick in the pants I needed to realize Mandy was the one for me. We were legally married in 2018 and had a fun ceremony in Las Vegas in March of 2019 that the Hydes attended.

It isn't easy with both Mandy and me in the military. However, I can't be mad at the Army because if we both hadn't been stationed in Germany at the same time we would have never met.

We chose Daniel for our son's middle name thinking of three very important Daniels in our lives. I had an Uncle Daniel who passed away when I was a teenager, and Mandy also had an Uncle Daniel who played a significant role in her life until he passed away from COVID, when the pandemic was very new. With Dan Hyde also being a significant friend in my life, Daniel (although a heavy name for us) also seemed to be the way to honor the three Daniels that are no longer with us but were greatly loved and cherished while they were.

Elliott will hear plenty of "Daniel" stories as he grows up and learns about the three Daniels he was named after.

ELLIOTT DANIEL KELLY was born on December 17, 2021, at Brooke Army Medical Center, San Antonio, TX, to James Brian (JB) and Mandy Kelly.

ASHLEY

When Ashley announced on social media her son's arrival in February of 2016, and his name Hudson Daniel, I recall making the comment to her that I loved his middle name. I did so to "acknowledge" the name Daniel, but hoping by doing so in the way I did, that I wouldn't be assuming anything. At that time, Ashley explained that Daniel was actually her husband's first name. He had always gone by Levi, but his legal name is Daniel Levi. When I told Ashley I had had no idea she said not many people knew. Therefore, I assumed Hudson's middle name was after his dad and his dad alone.

*Six years later, in February 2022, a second dear friend of Ashley's passed away very unexpectedly. Ashley mentioned in a comment on social media that she couldn't believe two of her best, favorite guy friends Daniel, and now Paul, have both passed. For some reason after reading that comment on social media and Ashley having just mentioned the 6th birthday of Hudson Daniel, I got a strong feeling I should ask Ashley about Hudson's middle name. I am so happy Ashley and I finally had a conversation and I learned that Hudson is named after **both** his dad and Daniel.*

Ashley's thoughts:

The name Daniel represents the type of man I admire and honor. A man who is selfless, kind, humble, strong, hardworking, generous, and handsome. Daniel has a heart of gold. He is the type of man I could only hope to raise. The world is a better place because of "Daniel."

My husband recently reminded me that I wanted to name Hudson, Daniel, but he was adamant that we use Hudson as our son's first name. I still call Hudson, "Daniel" a lot. He responds to Hudson, Hudson Daniel, and Daniel.

I met Daniel Hyde at La Loma Junior High School. He played baseball with my best friend, Katy Suzuki.

My earliest memories are of Daniel and me passing notes in our 7th grade science class. Daniel was my first junior high boyfriend. We later decided that friends was a better title for us.

Fast forward to high school: Daniel was the only boy ever allowed to come over to my house to visit.

I admired Daniel because he was kind to everyone, he treated everyone the same regardless of social status. He led by example, he had a smile that could light up a room. He was good at everything he did. I loved that Daniel never judged anyone and he always had an open ear to listen. He never hesitated to speak his mind diplomatically but was always polite and politically correct. Daniel was the most religious person I knew in high school, but you would never have known it. I loved that he never tried to push his beliefs on others or lecture them. He instead made a lasting impression on everyone with 1000% effort, tender words, always kind, and an outstanding, inclusive attitude. Daniel was "perfect." I used to joke with him and call him Daniel "**Hype**" because he was always the buzz at school. He would get embarrassed and say, "Ash, no I am not." **He was always so humble**. Daniel was something so special.

HUDSON DANIEL CHERRY was born on February 17, 2016, in Modesto, CA, to Levi and Ashley Da Silva-Cherry.

THINGS I'VE LEARNED

The greatest gifts I have received from putting this book together are the stories I didn't know and the relationships I have developed with the boys' parents and with Ben.

The blessing of each one of these precious namesakes has come to us in different ways as told in their unique story. The boys are not listed in age order because some parents could not or did not come forward immediately. Daniel's namesakes are introduced as we became aware of them and that is the way it was destined to be.

Over the past 13 years, each time I hear from a new soldier, friend, or classmate, or receive a picture I have never seen, I get the tiniest piece of Daniel back. I have learned so much about my son through the compiling of these stories.

Brian, Andrea, and I were always impressed with Daniel for his drive to do everything well, the attempt for perfection, and his energy and love of learning, leading, and being the guy everyone could count on. Continually we learn things we didn't know through his impact on others. Daniel left for West Point when he was 18 and spent very little time with us between ages 18-24. His West Point summers were spent in continued training. He took the minimal time between graduation and Officer training so he could "get it done." He was so ready for the work he had been trained to do and it seems like a whirlwind from his high school graduation to his death at barely 24.

Thankfully his friends have filled in many of the gaps. Saying I am grateful is an understatement. I treasure these stories, the people who tell them, the love within them, and the respect and honor continually given to Daniel by everyone who ever knew him.

No matter if the encounter with Daniel was literally 10 minutes or for his lifetime, people don't stop loving him. We could not be more grateful or more blessed.

My deepest thanks to everyone who helped me gather these beautiful stories and memories.

IMMORTALIZED IN INK

Right after Daniel was killed, I started talking about getting a tattoo on the inside of my wrist. A big cross with a purple heart and…I don't know…some message or quote. Luckily, Derek Cole, a calm force at that time, said repeatedly to me, "Just think about it. Why don't you wait on that? Give it some time."

I ended up with a small tattoo on my right hand. It is perfect and I love it. I waited 10 months. I thought about it long and hard. I even wrote it out with an ink pen so I could look at it and be sure. Thank you, Derek, for the sound advice.

I would say in general to anyone who loses someone important in your life, WAIT! Just wait! On everything! Don't get rid of their things too quickly, don't make life-altering decisions too fast. Just catch your breath and wait. After the first-year fog begins to clear, you will think better and your decisions will make more sense. It takes time.

And to those that say, "It will get easier," I say it does NOT. I think it gets more and more challenging the longer you are without that person, especially in the case of your child.

Thank you to the friends and family that chose to honor Daniel through body art.

On Daniel's 25th birthday, 10 months after his death, I went downtown and handed a card Daniel had sent me to a tattoo artist. I asked the artist if he could match Daniel's printing and told him I wanted my tattoo on my right hand.

After the artist repeatedly asked if I was SURE I wanted a tattoo on my hand, and I assured him I did, he proceeded. I chose my right hand so that when I salute the flag Daniel is there with me. I love seeing his name **in his own printing** every single day.

I recall walking out of the tattoo studio with a very sore and immediately bruised hand. I looked down at my one and only tattoo and thought shoot, the tail on the L is too long. Then I glanced at the card Daniel had signed and said to myself…no, it is perfect!

I was 51 when I got my first tattoo.

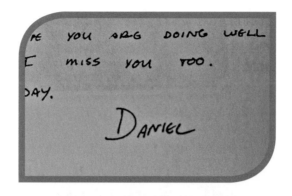

JON

Daniel was one of my favorite people growing up. He was always someone that I looked up to even though we only attended elementary school together. We played baseball together, he was the shortstop, and I played second and third base. We attended different junior high and high schools but would run into one another occasionally during our high school years.

After I saw the statue created for Daniel at Downey High School, I decided that is how I would pay my respects. I have a friend that is a tattoo artist and was thrilled to design this tattoo for me, in memory of Daniel.

BILLY

A Hyde family friend, and one of Daniel's high school football coaches and mentors.

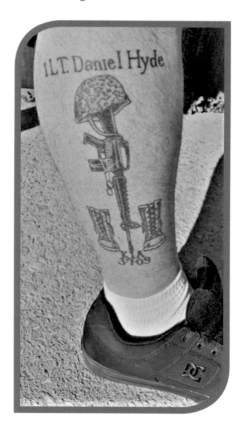

SCOTT

Daniel and I became good friends in high school. Another friend of ours, Paul, was the manager of a restaurant. A few of us guys would go to the restaurant, get food, and hang out.

Daniel treated everyone the same way, with respect. It didn't matter what social group you identified with; Daniel was friendly to everyone. I called Daniel "the golden child." Daniel always met every challenge head on and gave 100%. He never drank in high school. I always admired that Daniel didn't need to fit in. He marched to his own drummer.

I don't think Daniel realized all the girls were in love with him. I think he was oblivious...he was focused on his goals.

I was beyond crushed when I heard what happened to Daniel in Iraq. I honestly thought he would be the President one day.

NICOLE

I grew up with Daniel and Andrea. Our parents were friends, and we attended the same church. After Daniel died in Iraq, I wanted to get a tattoo to honor his memory.

God is our warrior looking over us and He is with Daniel who is looking over us as well.

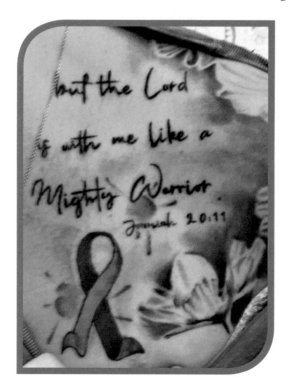

RILEY

On Riley's 18th birthday she got Daniel's birthdate in Roman numerals!

RENEE

My tattoo has a dual meaning. After finishing my first 50-mile race, which I believe Dan helped me complete in time, I got the running shoe sole showing 50 for 50. It represents 50 miles for my 50th birthday. The sole also forms the 1 in the number 13, in memory of my nephew, Daniel.

CHERYL

I have three tattoos honoring my nephew, Daniel. The ribbon on my left calf was my first. The second, located on my right wrist, is of a dumbbell with the number 13. The third, and my favorite, is located on my lower back.

It is difficult to say why people get memorial tattoos. Perhaps it is merely a means of carrying those memories and honoring those you love in quiet, special ways, for a lifetime.

EPILOGUE: LIFE SINCE THEN

Since serving as Dan's escort 13 years ago, a whole lot has obviously happened. The Army moved me six times. I deployed two more times. I got married. I had two kids. I became a homeowner. I accomplished everything I ever truly wanted to do in the Army, which included a stint at West Point teaching. I made it back to Hawaii, which is where I am currently stationed, albeit in a very different situation than when Dan and I romped around as young single Lieutenants preparing for war. I've more or less lived the "American Dream" while continuing to serve my country, and it's not lost on me that Dan never had a chance to experience any of these things.

Dan has been there along the way since I brought him home in March of 2009. Mostly indirectly, and often out of mind, but he has been a force in my life, nonetheless. How could he not be? His death was the first real trauma I had to deal with as an adult. It changed me and altered the direction of my life in ways known and unknown. Dan's death was never going to be something I was just going to move on from. As such, Dan's and my journey together did not come to an end on March 21, 2009, when I left Modesto. It merely changed.

When I returned to Hawaii in April 2009, following my escort duty, my adult life really got started. I settled into my new home on Oahu's North Shore and continued progression in what still felt like a very new career in the Army. In a short time, I received a promotion from platoon leader to company executive officer and would make the rank of Captain the following year. I didn't exactly love being in the Army, and the announcement of an upcoming deployment in summer 2010 didn't exactly thrill me, but I felt I was pretty good at it, and I enjoyed the camaraderie I had with the soldiers I served with.

Andrea and I became fast friends. Shortly after the Celebration of Life, we started texting on a regular basis. We talked about the general happenings in our lives, exchanged jokes, provided snarky commentary on pop culture, and generally just checked up on each other. It was nice to have conversations on things completely unrelated to Dan's death or the week of his funeral. Not that we didn't think about him, it's that he was no longer the only thing tying us together. We had our own relationship. While there was no way I could ever replace her brother, we became as close as family. Andrea even called me her BFF. We planned a visit and Andrea would come out to Hawaii that July. Moving forward we would typically see each other at least once a year.

About two months after my escort duty, I met my wife, Stephanie. I nearly messed things up a couple times in the lead up to our first date, but when it finally happened, we just worked. We had that connection where we could be our true selves hardly knowing each other. It was on that first date that I told Stephanie about Dan. When I told Stephanie about him, I did not mention much outside of him being a close friend who was killed in Iraq. I didn't talk about the escort experience or the hurt I was still feeling. Over time, Stephanie would learn all about Dan Hyde, and what he meant to me, as his story came out in bits and pieces over the course of our relationship. I wish she and Dan had met.

In late June of 2010, I deployed to Iraq for the second time. My unit deployed to the Saladin Province in northern Iraq and was based out of COP Speicher, just outside the city of Tikrit. We were about 50 miles away from Samarra where Dan got killed. It was kind of eerie to be operating around the same area as Dan, as if somehow it would lead us to share similar fates. The deployment would be a lot harder than my previous one. No single event was as difficult as taking Dan home, but things took their toll.

During this deployment, which lasted seven months, I would come under fire for the first time; I would feel that helplessness and guilt when one of your soldiers is seriously wounded and there's nothing you can do to take it back; two soldiers from my company would be killed, James McClamrock and

Phillip Jenkins; I would tell a soldier that his best friend had just been killed; and I would battle with a toxic emotional stew of anger, regret, hopelessness, apathy, and bitterness. It was a bad time in my life, yet I pushed through it as I had done in Modesto. As Dan had taught me, life must go on. And it did.

Despite me souring on the Army to an extent, I decided to stick around and elected to continue progressing in my career by attending the Captain's Career Course at Fort Benning, Georgia in March 2011. Stephanie came to Georgia with me. She took a huge chance, as we were only dating at the time, and I will be forever grateful that she did. We became engaged that summer.

The Career Course was the break I needed from the operational Army, and it reinvigorated my desire to serve. It was also a great place for reconnecting with friends and West Point classmates. My time there overlapped with many of my closest friends, and we had the opportunity to relive some of our West Point shenanigans, even if we were slightly more restrained. Despite the fun I had with my old friends, it saddened me that Dan would not be one of the friends I would link back up with. He was gone after all.

In the fall of 2011, Stephanie and I moved near Fort Campbell, Kentucky for my next assignment with the 101st Airborne Division. I would serve in the 2nd Battalion, 506th Infantry Regiment, nicknamed "Currahee" and made famous by their portrayal in the *Band of Brothers* mini-series. It was a dream come true. As an 18-year-old kid applying to West Point, I was inspired as I watched the exploits of the Paratroopers from the 506th. I wanted to be a Currahee and now that wish had come to fruition. It is something I am still proud of. It makes me wonder what unfulfilled dreams Dan had that he never had a chance to live out.

I served as a Currahee for close to three years where I started as an assistant operations officer on battalion staff and finished as the commander of Whiskey Company. I thoroughly enjoyed my time as a company commander. To this date, it is the best job I've had in the operational Army. I got to lead, train, and inspire soldiers on a daily basis, and I was fortunate to have a phenomenal group of men to work with. As part of my command philosophy, I included "Do not accept mediocrity in any aspect of your life," as a tribute to Dan, and as a source of inspiration for the company. Though Dan was gone, he could still lead and inspire others. As far as I was concerned, his spirit would live on in the company.

As things progressed in my professional life, they did so, too, in my personal life. On July 21, 2012, Stephanie and I were married in Nashville. We had an amazing wedding. It was just plain fun, and it was nice to have our closest friends and families there to attend. Glenda, Brian, and Andrea were all in attendance and I'm pretty sure they had a blast. Married now, I gained a new perspective on life. My life would now be a partnership and I would have someone to complement my journey through its ups and downs, which included the Army's plans.

While serving in command, I deployed for my third time, this time to Afghanistan in May 2013. Though it was a different country, it had a similar feel as the other deployments to Iraq. There were patrols in dusty towns amongst people you weren't sure of and who weren't sure of you, the camaraderie that comes with your fellow soldiers while living in an inhospitable area, the frustrations with superior officers and the mission, and that uneasy feeling that arises occasionally knowing that any day could be your last. While we had a couple close calls, everyone from my company made it home alive. Overall, my deployment to Afghanistan was a much more positive experience than the previous one to Iraq.

I returned home to Stephanie in late November 2013, and from that point it seemed like my life accelerated forward. Shortly after my return, Stephanie became pregnant with our first child. Having children is something we had always wanted, and we were about to enter a stretch where deployments would not be looming over us, so the timing could not have been better. I had been selected to return to West Point to teach history, and part of the assignment was to first attend graduate school to earn an advanced degree. I would still be in the Army, but I was now going down a very different path than the previous five years.

In the summer of 2014, we departed Fort Campbell and moved to Tucson, Arizona where I would attend the University of Arizona. Graduate school was a whole lot different than my undergrad experience at West Point and my time in the Army. I went from preparing for and serving in the wars in Iraq and Afghanistan, often responsible for the literal lives of others, to a whole lot of reading and writing and individual intellectual development. You would think things would be easier for me after three deployments in seven years, but the transition was quite difficult. It took me a full semester to get used to academia and an entire year to actually enjoy it. The growing pains with the shift in my professional life were only compounded by major changes in my personal life.

Shortly after I began my graduate work, my daughter, Mariel, was born. Her birth brought a seismic change to my outlook on life, which had not happened since perhaps Dan's death. Mariel, or Mari as we call her, became my priority, my focus, my purpose. There was this tiny little human, a literal part of me that I was now responsible for in every possible way. Her entry into the world expanded my emotions in a way where I could be positively smitten with my new love while also being terrified by the multitude of dangers that could harm my baby at any moment for the rest of her life. Parenting brings about so many emotions, it's hard to put into words, but if you're a parent you know what I'm talking about.

Parenting had changed a lot of things including my perspective on serving as Dan's escort. I now had an even greater appreciation for Brian and Glenda. As a parent now, I couldn't imagine losing a child. It became my greatest fear. I don't know how I would go on if I lost a child and Brian and Glenda had to live that. They had to move on from losing their baby. I know it is something that still pains them to this day, but I remain in awe of their strength and resilience. They also helped me realize that I would never be able to protect Mari from everything. The best I could do would be to raise my child to be a good person, like Dan. The Hydes had knocked it out of the park in that aspect and provided me with an additional source of inspiration as I fought through the parenting trenches.

In the fall of 2015, I found out that my role as a parent would expand. Stephanie became pregnant for a second time with our son. Since Dan's death, my plan had always been to have Daniel somewhere in my son's name. Had Mari been a boy, her name would have been Grant Daniel, named after two of my heroes, obviously Dan and former President and General-in-Chief of the U.S. Army during the Civil War, Ulysses S. Grant. Due to another tragedy involving a young man who we lost far too soon, that plan changed.

In December of 2014, Stephanie's cousin Zach tragically died in a car accident at the age of 19. Stephanie was absolutely crushed. Zach was a great kid with his entire life ahead of him. Like with Dan, his fate was cruelly unfair, and the world seemed slightly worse off with him being gone. When we found out we'd be having a son, Stephanie approached me about having his middle name be Zachary instead of Daniel. I agreed. There were already several new kids with Daniel as their namesake, but none for Zach. Like Dan, Zach needed to be properly honored and, in my heart, I knew that Dan would have wanted us to recognize Zach over himself. So, my son would be Grant Zachary. Despite not having Daniel anywhere in Grant's name, he would still be intimately connected to Dan. We asked Andrea to serve as Grant's godmother and she accepted.

Between graduate school and parenting, our two years in Tucson flew by. The break from the Army was admittedly a nice change of pace, though I stayed pretty busy between my studies and taking care of an infant. The next stop was West Point, where I would put my new degree to use while developing the future officers of the Army. After two years of intensive graduate studies, I was excited about getting back to the Army, even if the soldiering I would be doing would be in the classroom instead of the field.

I returned to West Point in the summer of 2016. The academy was similar to what I remembered, though I was very different from the 18-year-old kid who arrived in the summer of 2003. I was a husband, a father of two (Grant would be born about a month after we arrived), a senior Captain, and a combat veteran. Being back created this weird feeling where it almost felt like I had never left despite all that had changed, including the fate of some of my classmates like Dan. My return was a class reunion of sorts, and once again it occurred to me that this could have been another time to reunite with Dan had things gone differently.

My three years teaching at West Point were my most fulfilling years in the Army. Since graduating from West Point, returning to the academy to teach was something I had always planned on if I stayed in the Army. I wanted to give back to the institution that made me into the man I am and connect with the next generation of Army officers. It was my opportunity to mentor future officers into becoming better than I ever was; to be like Dan. On the first lesson of every class I taught, 22 in total, I posted a slide with a picture of Dan and me from our cadet days and the quote, "Do not accept mediocrity in any aspect of your life." That's over 350 cadets that received Dan's marching orders.

During an academic trip I led to Hawaii with a group of cadets, we visited Dan's old unit at Schofield Barracks and stopped at a memorial plaque with his name inscribed. I opened up to the cadets about who Dan was, how much he was respected, and what he meant to me. During this instruction my voice cracked as I became overwhelmed by emotion. In the Army you often assume roles based on the position you're in. With my cadets I typically tried to combine the professional demeanor expected of mid-grade officers with a hint of sarcasm, and to come off as somewhat of a hard ass. The veneer was gone. I was vulnerable in front of these young men and women and upon reflection I'm glad they saw me that way. I showed them what Dan meant to me, to all of us, and that the profession they all volunteered to join had real consequences. I told Dan's story, imparting who he was in the slightest way on the next generation of Army officers. One of the cadets, someone who could always be kind of a wise ass, came up after my impromptu speech and thanked me.

While at West Point, I gained additional clarity about the things that mattered most to me. I became ever more certain with the prioritization of my family over all else. You get a lot of family time at West Point, and it's something I came to expect. I was home before dinner nearly every night and did not have the extended absences that come with typical Army assignments. Stephanie and I grew together as husband and wife, and parents, and I got to watch my children grow, not having to worry about an extended deployment that would have me miss a relatively sizeable portion of their lives. I also realized that my favorite part of being in the Army was not soldiering but mentoring those in my charge. I established an extremely close relationship with a handful of cadets who I've had the privilege to watch become fine young officers. My career didn't exactly take a back seat, but I was more certain in what I wanted to get out of it.

I loved teaching at West Point, but it couldn't last forever. After three years it was time to get back to the operational Army, or the "real" Army as some might say. My next assignment would be with the famed 82nd Airborne Division at Fort Bragg, North Carolina. Now a Major, I was entering the part of my career where the workload and responsibility dramatically increased. Some use the term "Iron Major" to describe it. The idyllic life the family and I lived at West Point would now give way to the fast pace, long days, and occasional unpredictability of traditional Army life. In the summer of 2019, we bought a house and moved to North Carolina for the next chapter.

Going from a teacher concerned with instructing cadets on history, to an operations officer responsible for the training and readiness of a battalion of 700 paratroopers was quite a shock to the system. It was a difficult transition to say the least and I was pretty miserable at first, to be honest. The joy I found in teaching did not translate to the new job, and I had far less time with my family, especially the children who would be in bed by the time I got home on some nights. It didn't help that I never really projected what I wanted out of my career after West Point. I questioned whether staying in the Army was the right choice and even began doubting my abilities, a first in my career. Through it all, Stephanie stood by and encouraged me. Her support and the knowledge that my work supported her, and the children helped me through and carry on.

After a rocky start as a major in the 82nd Airborne, I found my rhythm. It was a busy time in my career, but I came to appreciate the new role I assumed in the Army working at a higher organizational level, where I was more detached from what was going on at the soldier level. My role gave me the opportunity to have a larger impact in my battalion, serving as the number three and then number two officer in the unit, and I continued finding the most satisfaction in mentoring the officers and enlisted soldiers below me. Like my cadets, they too received Dan's marching orders to not accept mediocrity. I also got to serve as a paratrooper and jump out of airplanes, which is something I dreamed of doing as a senior in high school. It could be a bumpy ride, but I had found my place again.

Despite many long days, week to month long training exercises, and nights away from home, I never ended up deploying. I was supposed to deploy, to Iraq again, but the COVID-19 pandemic changed all that and I didn't end up going. Stephanie didn't mind and honestly, neither did I. Going into harm's way is part of the job, and something I'm still ready to do, but as I've grown older and become a husband and a father, it's not something I necessarily want to do. I learned early in my career that no one is invincible. The thought of my children growing up fatherless or my wife being a widow are things I don't want to seriously contemplate if I don't have to. Nonetheless, if duty calls, I will be there.

My time in the 82nd Airborne Division came and went. And after two fast and furious years at Fort Bragg, we found ourselves back to where it all started. In the summer of 2021, we moved back to Oahu, Hawaii where I took a staff job working at the United States Army Pacific headquarters at Fort Shafter. There's a certain sentimentality that came with moving back to Hawaii. It's where I started my adult years that set my entire life in motion. Adding to that sentimentality is that I now get to raise my family here. We bought a house which incidentally is about a mile from the church Dan, and I went to all those years ago, and the church is right next to the kids' school. The house has a lanai – or balcony as a Mainlander would call it – that overlooks the ocean and downtown Honolulu. We have settled in nicely and it feels like we're home with the knowledge that the Army will make some other place home in a few years. Calling it paradise is a bit of an exaggeration when you actually live in Hawaii, though it sure is nice.

Being back in Hawaii has also afforded me more time to reflect on my experience with Dan. It was our last time together when he was alive, and the sights of Oahu often bring back fond memories of us. And as the children have grown older, I've been able to share things about Dan with them. My daughter first found out about Dan when she inquired about the KIA bracelet I wear etched with Dan's name, the date of his death, and where he was killed. When Mari asked about it, I told her it was to remember my friend who was killed in the war by bad guys. I kept it simple knowing we'll have a more nuanced conversation about things at some point in the future. During one discussion about Dan's death, which included my own participation in the Iraq war and how I never got hurt by bad guys, my daughter commented, *"You were lucky."* Her words struck a chord; such a straightforward and profound statement about the nature of war coming from a seven-year-old. It's a statement that got me thinking long and hard about the way my life turned out compared to Dan's.

After Dan's death and my time as his escort, I pledged to honor his legacy and be more like him. Have I done that? Lord knows I'm far from perfect: I'm still quick to anger; I've phoned it in at work because I just didn't feel like putting the extra effort in; I've been too hard on my children, especially my son; I've been selfish and lazy and cynical and insecure; and I've accepted mediocrity over and over again over the past 13 years because quite frankly it was acceptable given the situation, and easier. Have I actually lived Dan's legacy? I don't know. Maybe the point was never to not be mediocre, but to be better versions of ourselves and encourage others to do the same, and to see the best in people, even if they might not deserve it. I think I've done that.

I guess when it all comes down to it, Dan's legacy is more than just me. Dan lived a full life, and he continues to live on through everyone he's touched, directly and indirectly, in big and small ways. That's the ultimate legacy of my friend, Dan Hyde. He inspired us in life and continues to inspire us in death. He was and is a larger-than-life figure, despite his modesty and attempts to act like he was just a regular dude. He continues to live in all of us – in me, Glenda, Brian, Andrea, all the new Daniels, in Mariel and Grant Zachary, in Stephanie, and even the young officers who never met him. In an abstract way, perhaps Dan is more alive today than he was 13 years ago on that last patrol.

Standing out on my lanai, looking off into the Pacific Ocean, I still can't help but think about what could've been, what 13 additional years of life would have brought Dan. A wife? Children? A nice house? Fulfillment? Would he be on the fast track to general or President as many of us had speculated? Obviously, he would be crushing it in the Army if he were still in, coming up on battalion command before his peers. The possibilities seem endless. So much has happened in my life since I brought Dan back to Modesto, and he never got the chance to have similar experiences. Maybe I am *lucky*. Even if that's so, I will continue to do my best to not take it all for granted – to honor Dan by spreading his message and carrying myself as he would. I am part of Dan Hyde's legacy, as is my family, and despite the pain that still lingers from his death, there's something comforting about that.

Charlie Mike

Printed in the United States
by Baker & Taylor Publisher Services